THE COUNTRY WITHIN

THE COUNTRY WITHIN

NEIL SWAN

Maclean Dubois

This edition first published in hardback in Great Britain
in 2018 by Maclean Dubois
14/2 Gloucester Place, Edinburgh EH3 6EF

ISBN: 978-0-9565278-8-2

British Library Cataloguing-in-Publication Data
A catalogue record for this book is available on request
from the British Library.

Designed and typeset in Garamond by Abigail Salvesen.
Printed and bound by Gutenberg Press Ltd, Malta.

For my mother Nancie

Within each of us is a country made up of memories of people and places. That country within is our country for the whole of our lives.

ACKNOWLEDGEMENTS

I would like to acknowledge the considerable help I have had in bringing this book to publication.

Alexander McCall Smith has encouraged me to write and with great generosity has attended to all the processes of publication. In all the years that he has been a friend, I have observed that few things give him more pleasure than helping others develop their talents. The greatest compliment he has paid me, has been not to shrink from telling me what I would rather not have heard – usually that what I had written was not my voice. Without him, my writing would have remained on my hard drive.

Nicky Wood, my editor, excised paragraphs that followed my obsessions and would have appalled or bored readers.
Keith and Colin Risk and my brother Alasdair were kind enough to read an early draft and made careful comments which supported the judgements that Nicky subsequently made.

Alison Roberts illustrated the route of my mother's flight from Burma.

My father Norman and my maternal grandmother Kathleen were a great help posthumously for having written down with honesty and clarity, their experiences of living in what was then called 'the East'.

Finally, my mother Nancie was the mother elephant who remembers everything. She was prepared to answer questions about personal matters that are frequently left unasked because they seem impertinent, but which can give a key to understanding.

CHAPTER 1

Burma

Should a memoir begin at birth? If a memoir is supposed to be an account based on personal knowledge, the description of an event about which one can have no possible recollection would seem to be an immediate breach of trust. Granted there are people who claim to remember their births, but they live on the edge of sanity.

The benefit of starting in the delivery room, either in hospital or at home with jugs of hot water and towels, is that it gives context for the person's life. Did they take the silver spoon, melt it down, squander the cash and end up destitute, or did they rise to great heights, having been born to a poor unmarried mother uncertain of her child's paternity? True the account will be hearsay, but it is still part of the influence that helps to shape us.

The question, though, is whether the delivery room is early enough. To say that you were born in a particular place is no more interesting than saying that a Mars Bar is made in Slough. You want to know, why Slough? What was it that appealed to Forrest Mars back in 1932? Was Slough somewhere he could find people with relevant research and development skills? Was it because Slough was near a large market in London? Did a site become available with an existing factory which Forrest could adapt? Once you know the answer to the question, Slough stops being a fact and becomes a story.

I was born in Burma, a country to which my parents had come by very different routes.

My father, Norman Swan, was a Scot who had grown up in Peterhead, a fishing village in the north-east of Scotland where my grandfather, Douglas, an Irishman from the north and a minister in the Church of Scotland, had charge of a parish for over fifty years.

As a preacher, Douglas was an imposing figure. He filled the pulpit with his tall, broad frame and had the useful asset of an Ulsterman's penetrating accent, though fortunately in his case he had lost the indignation that can turn an Ulsterman's mildest observation into a final demand. Instead he had evolved a style of speaking that suggested he was on the edge of a deep belly chuckle.

For all his amiability, there was a darker side to him. When, in his twenties, he had boarded a ship to Scotland, he had made sure to take with him his cherished prejudices against Catholics, even sharing them with my grandmother, Lizzie, a sweet Edinburgh lady educated at George Watson's, a school whose pupils prided themselves on the perfection of their gentility. Unlike his intolerance, hers never rang true. When she talked of Catholics breeding like rabbits and having shifty eyes, it was as unconvincing as the lashes of a seaman ordered to flog a friend.

The people of Peterhead do not appear to have demanded much from their minister beyond a reassuring benevolence.

*Douglas with his children in height order; Norman, Dodie,
Norah and Harold*

Long after Douglas retired, Norman found a tin trunk
which contained every sermon he had ever preached, neatly
wrapped up in quarterly bundles and tied with pink tape,
like title deeds to property. In the hope that they might give
some insight into the social changes that had occurred in the
first half of the twentieth century, Norman read them, but
discovered they contained little more than pious platitudes.
Not even the world wars merited a mention. His ability
to shield his congregation from unpleasantness might well
have explained his popularity.

Norman must have had a happy childhood, though I
infer that on the same basis that I might conclude that a
house that is still standing has good foundations. He was a
balanced adult, comfortable in his skin, and he never
harboured any grudges about his upbringing. Whenever
he gathered with his siblings, they reminisced in the light-

hearted way of people who had been content with their friends, their community and each other.

At the local school, he was fortunate to be in a year of bright pupils. A distant cousin was married to a senior Scottish judge who encouraged him to apply for a scholarship to Fettes College in Edinburgh. The scholarship, which he sat for and won, was available only to boys from state schools and covered the cost of the fees and the uniform.

The transition to the private school system went smoothly, though he had to adjust to a world without girls, and his

Norman (right) at Fettes College

north-eastern accent made him conspicuous. During an English lesson in his first term, the class was asked what punctuation mark should be inserted to show words written in parentheses. When he replied, 'A curly bracket,' rolling the 'r's as he spoke, the class dissolved in laughter.

Soon his accent was blended with standard English to became that of a high caste Scot; sufficiently anglicised to establish his standing while retaining the trace Scots necessary to protect his egalitarian credentials.

After Fettes, he went first to Edinburgh University to read classics and then to Peterhouse College, Cambridge to read History. In his final term, he obtained two job offers; one from Tootal Ties and the other from the Burmah Oil Company. Fearing he might sound ridiculous if he had to tell his friends he had a job with the former, he headed to Burma, a country Douglas struggled to find on the map.

He spent a month travelling out by ship, eking out the meagre five pounds of expenses that the company had advanced, my grandfather not having thought to add to it. His first hint at the subtle social gradations of life out East came on the day of departure when, in a crowded passageway, a woman declared loudly that there was positively no one on board.

At Simon Artz store in Port Said, he went ashore wearing a trilby hat and a grey suit and emerged with prickly heat powder, thin cotton pyjamas, a specific against dysentery, sunglasses and a khaki coloured solar topi.

Within the first week of arriving in Rangoon, he had rooms in a shared bachelor house or 'chummery', a third-hand Plymouth motor car and driver, a servant and a rich sporting and social life largely centred on the club, but which also included the racy 'Silver Grill' nightclub.

As a single man, he was sent on assignments up country and developed friendships with Burmese and Indians, in the process earning the nickname 'Abnorm'. Unwisely, at a public meeting of expatriates he let his feelings be known about the ban on Burmese and Indians joining the two main European clubs, the Pegu and the Gymkhana. He was duly dressed down by the General Manager for providing 'political ammunition' to agitators and feared he might be sent home. To his relief, as he rose to leave the room, the General Manager told him not to take the carpeting too seriously and that his attitude might well be right.

Norman's graduation from Cambridge University

Before the war, it was safe to walk anywhere in the country and at weekends they would set off to the jungle, climbing mountains and returning to Rangoon from a wayside station on the night train. To a boy from the north-east of Scotland, the smell of woodsmoke at dawn, the sound of cocks crowing at dawn and the stirring of jungle life in the brief cool before the heat of the day rolled in, were as exciting as they were alien. He was mesmerised and utterly infatuated.

After the fall of Singapore, when it became clear that the oil installations were likely to fall into the hands of the Japanese, Norman helped destroy them.

Without a job and aware of his duty, he joined the army for the duration of the war. As a soldier, he will not have been a great asset as he had a gentle nature, though one day that changed.

He had developed a close friendship with a fellow officer who came from a town near to Peterhead. When they were heard talking to each other in their local dialect, the Doric, it was decided that they could be used to pass messages in a semi-secure form over the radio. If the British troops had no idea what they were saying, it was unlikely that the Japanese would.

One day, on a patrol, Norman came across his friend's severed head on the parapet of a bridge. From that moment on he wanted to kill.

Before he could commit some reckless act of revenge, he was hit on the head by a long wooden pole during a training exercise and invalided away from front line duties to recover from severe concussion and loss of memory. Until the end of hostilities, he was stationed in India working on a programme for the post-war reconstruction of Burma.

After VJ day, he re-joined the Burmah Oil Company in Rangoon and set about repairing the damage he had helped cause to its plant three years earlier.

My mother's history of how she came to be in Burma at the end of the war had more twists and turns. Like me, Nancie was born there but had spent her years between birth and courtship mostly in England.

Her father, Val Powell, was a railway engineer. Privately educated as a day boy at Harrow School, he had left secondary education without going to university. His ambition was to complete an engineering apprenticeship at the railway works at Crewe, but his father wanted him to work in a bank. They came to an arrangement, normally the stuff of novels, whereby Val would work in the bank for two years but would be free to start an apprenticeship if he found the prospect of easy riches disagreeable. At the end of the trial period, he turned his back on wealth.

After completing his training, he had to choose between job offers from Tanganyika Railways and Burma Railways. As neither company had a name that sounded ridiculous, he was forced to spin a coin. It fell for Burma Railways Company, an outcome he consolidated by marrying the daughter of a director of the company shortly after he arrived there.

In 1924, Nancie was born in Mandalay, a city which at that time still had a splendour that matched its name, the British not yet having bombarded it; and she remained in Burma until she was sent to boarding school in England, aged five. For more than a decade, she saw her parents only every three or four years when they returned to England on leave. She did not go back to Burma until December

1940 when she sailed with her younger sister, Daphne, and brother, Dennis, on the *Stratheden*, a recently launched liner that had been converted for use as a troop carrier.

The moat round the Palace of Mandalay.
Photograph taken by Val Powell

Aged sixteen, she was old enough to know the danger posed by U-Boats but was reassured by the convoy's evasive zig-zag course and by the destroyers that busied themselves dropping depth charges. Had she known that the Admiralty codes were routinely being broken by the Germans who had advance warning of nearly every convoy's course, and had she realised that the U-Boats could not easily be detected, she might not have been as relaxed as she was in her cabin below the waterline.

The presence of the ship's orchestra gave a comforting illusion of peace; the crooner sang of nightingales in Mayfair; and passengers dressed up as if for the Ritz.

The young men on board were a distraction too at the morning dances, which were the only ones to which Nancie was entitled to go, evening dances being for First Class passengers only.

The convoy made its way across the Atlantic, soon leaving the protection of the Sunderland flying boats, and sailed down the east coast of the United States before crossing back to Sierra Leone where it paused to refuel before heading on to Cape Town and Bombay.

On arrival at Bombay, Nancie travelled by train across India to Calcutta where she boarded a Qantas Empire Class flying boat, the *Coorong* (VH-ABE), on the River Hooghly and flew to Rangoon with a single stop at Akyab.

At the end of the second leg of the flight, she glimpsed the gold of the Shwedagon Pagoda as they turned to make the final approach before alighting on the Rangoon River in a cloud of rainbowed spray. At the quayside, she stepped from the airline launch into the arms of her parents, and collapsed, exhausted.

The following year was blissful. There might have been war in Europe and anxiety about Japan's intentions, but Burma was still at peace and Val had been posted to MyitNge, a remote place accessible only on foot or by rail, where goods vehicles and passenger coaches were sent for repair.

There was no blackout and no rationing. For the first time since the age of five, Nancie experienced family life, walking in the countryside, identifying birds using the helpfully titled book *Birds of Burma* and swimming in the unpainted concrete pool that Val had built, funding its construction by issuing shares to friends and using a decommissioned First Class carriage as a changing room. For a while she became interested in architecture and considered enrolling to study it at Rangoon University, until she discovered that it did not have a faculty of architecture.

Daphne, Nancie, Kathleen and Dennis at MyitNge

After the disgrace of Singapore in February 1942, nervousness of the Japanese turned to fear. Val prepared the family for evacuation to India as refugees, insisting that they cram all their worldly possessions into a single suitcase. He himself was determined to stay until the last possible moment in order to keep the railways running.

The suitcase contained mainly clothes and sensible shoes, but each family member was allowed to put in a treasured object. Nancie chose a Chinese enamelled hairbrush and mirror she had been given the previous Christmas. My grandmother, Kathleen, packed the children's birth certificates and her marriage certificate together with six silver teaspoons which, in addition to their strong sentimental value, also had a value that could be weighed. Before she left the house, she removed the marriage certificate and left it for Val on his desk. Why she did so she could never explain, but it was a deliberate act.

The family bade farewell to Val twice. The first time they left the house to fly from Magwe airfield but were forced to return after it was bombed. The second time, a few days later, they took the train from Mandalay to Shwebo airfield, not travelling in the luxury of their usual inspection carriage coupled to the end of the train, but in Third Class, the hard seats a reminder of their changed status. It was a calendar month since the surrender of Singapore.

On arrival at the transit camp, refugees had their names added to a list and waited in huts where they sat on mats which demarcated each family's territory. Everyone was flown off in the order of their position on the list. The list could not be jumped. The list would not negotiate. The list could not be bribed. The list was inviolable. The list kept the peace.

On the fourth day, Kathleen was awoken to find an Air India Airspeed Envoy had arrived with the mail. After being weighed with their luggage, the family were told they could take the flight, though one of them had to sit on a cushion as there were only three seats for passengers.

When they landed at Chittagong, the pilot told them that the small aircraft had been operating at the limit of its range. There had been little fuel left in reserve.

They were taken to a club which had been turned into an evacuation centre. The following morning, they caught a train to Chandpur where they boarded a river steamer to take them upriver to a railway connection at Goalanda. As they scrambled up the bank from the ferry terminal to reach the station, they were smothered by a sandstorm which added a biblical feel to their flight. From Goalanda they took the train to Calcutta and spent the night in a convent. There was no food and no water for the bathrooms or lavatories, the hand-pumped water tanks having run dry, but there were rows of camp beds. Exhausted, they slept.

The following morning a member of the Evacuation Committee, set up to maintain order in a chaotic situation, asked Kathleen if she knew anyone in Calcutta. She gave the name of some friends; a phone call was made, and they were taken in as guests. Val had transferred money from his bank in Rangoon to Grindlays in Calcutta, so they now had shelter, food and cash. Although still refugees with an uncertain future, they had escaped immediate danger and were able to catch their breath.

Through the Evacuation Committee, Kathleen was able to establish that her sister-in-law, Dulcie, and infant son, Colin, had escaped and were in Calcutta, though her brother, Cyril, remained in Burma. The two women made contact and resolved that the families would stay together.

My mother's family could not remain with their friends for more than a few days as the house would be needed by other refugees. Dulcie recalled that her husband Cyril had enjoyed a stay at Dehradun, over a thousand miles away in the foothills of the Himalayas. On the basis of this slender recommendation, Kathleen contacted a Thomas Cook agent who booked rooms for them at the Savoy Hotel in Mussoorie, a town near Dehradun, though higher in the mountains. They arrived on 1 April, just two weeks after leaving their home in Burma, and immediately started to look for permanent accommodation.

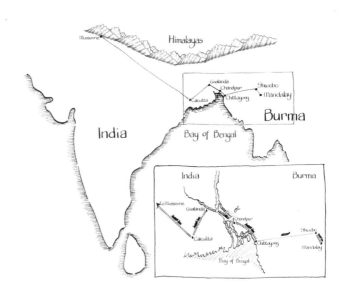

The evacuation route from Burma

An experienced traveller might be wary of any hotel called the Savoy that did not have a postal address in the Strand. While the rooms of the Mussoorie Savoy were comfortable and had views of snow-capped peaks, often brilliant against a clear blue sky, the food was dismal, consisting of re-cooked meat and little else, there being no cultivable ground in the area. Kathleen's complaints now seem petty set against the

14

suffering of those interned by the Japanese, but she did not yet realise that the iceberg had been hit.

The next weeks were taken up finding somewhere to live. All the while Kathleen worried about the plight of Val and Cyril as news seeped out about the evacuation of Mandalay and the advance of the Japanese.

Her misery came to an end unexpectedly when Val rang her, triumphant that he had finally tracked her down and explaining that he too was in Mussoorie.

Compared with others, he had been fortunate, though his escape had not been without alarm. He had been told by those in charge of the evacuation that because he had a double hernia, he had the right to fly out on one of the RAF or USAAF Dakotas that were shuttling officials and refugees to Assam. However, he had found it impossible to obtain a seat because others kept appearing who were deemed to have a greater need than he. Fortunately, a Chinese airliner made an unexpected refuelling stop on its way to Calcutta. A seat was available, albeit at a price that reflected the fact that he would be buying his life. He bought it without hesitation.

Cyril succeeded in escaping overland. For three weeks he had survived on half a cigarette tin of rice per day, a little Bovril and weak tea. A week after he arrived in India, he died from cerebral malaria.

His widow's trip back to England was as remarkable an escape as his own and might go some way to explaining why after the war ended, for many of their generation the height of tolerable excitement was to drive to the coast and read the Sunday papers.

Dulcie and her baby son Colin sailed from Bombay on the *SS Cairo*. On 6 November 1942, while on passage from

Cape Town to Brazil, the ship was brought to a stop by a torpedo fired by a U-Boat on the surface.

The U-Boat's commander, Karl-Friedrich Merten, waited while the passengers took to the lifeboats before firing the torpedoes that sank the ship. Speaking through a megaphone, he offered to take on board the submarine anyone who wanted to be interned, but his offer was declined. Before departing he added to their supplies and pointed out that they were two thousand miles from Brazil, one thousand miles from Africa and five hundred miles from St Helena. His final words were, 'Goodnight. Sorry for sinking you.' Unlike most of the U-Boat commanders, Karl-Friedrich Merten survived the war, living until he was eighty-seven. He deserved to enjoy every day of his life.

Dulcie and Colin spent two weeks in an open boat before being rescued by fishermen off St Helena, severely sunburned and desperate for water. Not everyone in the boat survived.

Meanwhile, in the calm of India, Nancie joined the Women's Auxiliary Army and ended the war in Delhi when victory was declared over Japan.

You might expect that as the clouds of war were blown away, Norman and Nancie, both now in India, would meet, their eyes locking in burning intensity, knowing that they had each found the soulmate for whom in some unspoken way they had been searching all their lives. You would be disappointed.

Nancie didn't help the speed of the narrative when in January 1946 she became engaged to a man who was a printer with the Baptist Missionary Press in Delhi. A month later she sailed to England with her parents, leaving him behind. She broke off her engagement by letter that autumn. She has no recollection of the moment she let the envelope slip from her fingers into the pillar box. She said he was dull, but not to remember pulling the trigger on the relationship shows an uncharacteristic callousness.

In the middle of the severe winter of 1947, Nancie travelled back to Burma with her family on a ship that left from Glasgow. After a thirty-hour rail journey from London during which the train was frequently brought to a halt by snow, she found herself sitting next to a woman of her own age on the coach that took them to the quay where their ship was moored. The woman was to become a lifelong friend. It was she who introduced my parents to each other after a rugby match in which Norman had been playing. Covered in sweat and dust, he must have stirred her feelings more than a printer of Baptist missionary tracts.

There was one final hurdle to be cleared. After VJ Day, Norman had been given home leave for a month. As soon as he was ashore, he had made contact with a teacher he had met in 1937 when he had been in his final year at Cambridge and with whom he had corresponded throughout the war. He had to move quickly, having only a little month. Within a week they were engaged and days later they were married.

The wedding night turned out to be a disaster and his bride discovered that, in the language of the day, she did not like men. It was a terrible blow to both of them. She remained in Britain while he returned to Burma. Norman had no desire to hurt her which made the apparent irrationality of her decision not to travel out with him hard to explain, as it exacerbated the embarrassment and humiliation.

In the gentlest of ways and with great sadness, they sought a divorce, though to obtain one they knew the law required one of them to admit having done something wrong. That fiction was satisfied by her agreeing to have deserted the marriage.

Norman only talked to me of his first marriage once, when I was fifteen. He had waited until then because he was worried that at a younger age I might in some way have been disturbed by the revelation. For that reason, he had also chosen a year in which I was not sitting an external exam. He need not have worried. He was talking of

Norman and Nancie's marriage at the Scots Kirk Rangoon

a person I did not know. If I felt any emotion, it was love for a man who could still describe his ex-wife as intelligent and highly attractive.

The divorce was granted in November 1948 and a month later my parents were married in the Scots Kirk in Rangoon.

A year later my elder brother, Alasdair, arrived. Two years after that my sister, Deborah, was born. Two years after that it was my turn to clip on the umbilical cord, wait for the green light and descend.

Nancie (holding Neil), May May and Norman. In the foreground, Alasdair and Deborah.

We left Burma before I developed the ability to remember anything, though I was often reminded that I was baptised by the Bishop of Rangoon, as if episcopal involvement was recognition of an elevated status.

Although I passed through it like a sleeper train in the night, Burma remains the land of my birth, the place I write on immigration forms. I have even learned to call it Myanmar, though Yangon is a step too far.

CHAPTER 2

India

From Rangoon we moved to Digboi in Assam, a town where oil had been found in the final years of the nineteenth century, not as the result of careful survey and test drilling, but in the way that water makes itself known in a flood. So close was the oil to the surface that it turned mud black when it was churned by elephants' feet as they worked on construction projects. As if the visual clue was not enough, the smell was overpowering.

It is not clear how Digboi acquired its name. Many believe it derives from the words shouted by an English engineer to exert the local labourers to greater efforts as they dug to find the source of the oil. If true, its continued use is an eternal reproach. Others argue that if oil flows to your feet, you have no need to coerce others to find it, though they offer no alternative suggestion as to how the name came into being.

When we first arrived, we lived in a brick-built house, but the chimney collapsed in an earthquake and destroyed it. The earthquake is possibly my first memory because I remember the strange feeling of lying on the grass as the ground moved under me.

We moved to Bungalow 51 which looked onto the golf course. In India, a bungalow was understood to be a house occupied by a single family and there was no assumption that it should be built on a single storey and filled with a pensioner.

Ours was two storeys high and of standard earthquake-proof design with a metal frame and thin timber walls. There were covered verandas on both floors, so deep and broad that, viewed from the side, they gave the house the profile of a capital letter 'E'. At the back of the house, connected by a covered pathway, was the cookhouse, a place to which bearers hastened to and fro, but to which I never went.

By day, the weather was sunny and warm, and at night the rain often pounded on the corrugated iron roof above my bedroom, as thunder crashed, lightning flickered, and the electricity supply failed. I used to look forward to these dramatic events as I lay in my bed, safely under my mosquito net. On quiet nights, I would ask to go downstairs to look at the white moon flowers which twined round supporting pillars of the balcony and opened magically after dark.

Once, I was awoken by my mother and taken by the light of a torch to a Land Rover parked outside our house. In the back of the vehicle lay a tiger that had just been shot, its tail hanging out of the back. It had been troubling local villagers and the man who was now showing us his trophy had been asked to kill it. I was invited to lift its tail to feel its weight, but even in death the creature overawed me, and I dared not touch it.

If I was timid, Alasdair caused consternation when he was seen by Nancie stroking a krait, a deadly snake. Speaking calmly, she told him to leave the nice snake alone and come to her. The snake was dead, but from that moment on we children were put through what was called 'snake drill'. If we saw a snake, we were to leave it alone and call a servant who would come along with a machete and chop it into hundreds and hundreds of little pieces. I never did see a snake though I saw plenty of their sloughed off skins in the garden near the swing; a warning that I was on their turf.

Between the house and the golf course we had a swimming pool little bigger than a rubbish skip, made of rough, unpainted concrete. Deborah and I would run naked round the garden and then jump in to cool off. There were always frogs in the water which, to shrieks from Deborah, I would catch in my hands and put into the grass, my first experience of having a skill that others valued.

I have no memory of Alasdair at that time because he was rarely at home. At the age of five he had been sent as a boarder to a pre-prep school in Winchester. It had been recommended by a friend and was also conveniently close to Lymington where my maternal grandparents had retired by the sea.

Deborah and I were looked after by our nanny called May May, a Karen from the south-east of Burma who had first worked for us in Rangoon. She was a loving woman and had a daughter in Burma whom she had to leave behind to be brought up by her grandmother. My parents never knew if May May had a husband. In the six years she lived with us, she never gave away the slightest clue and no one asked.

My personal debt to May May is possibly great. There was at one point an epidemic of polio in the area and a boy in a nearby house had caught it, suffering dreadfully. May May detected that I had a fever and put me to bed at once. She and Nancie nursed me carefully and I recovered to full health. Although I will never know if her prompt action influenced the outcome, the fact that she was credited with saving me from permanent injury is a testament to the love our family had for her and their relief at my full recovery.

On Sundays we went to the club, where there was a Sunday school. If there was any spiritual instruction, it was less memorable than the paper cones of peanuts we were given before going through to the club dining room to watch Tom and Jerry cartoons projected onto a screen rigged up on a table. Later we would use the club swimming pool where I would jump fearlessly off the top board, especially if someone was racing up the ladder to save me from myself.

From time to time we would set off with friends in a convoy of cars and drive out into the jungle to walk across rope bridges, ride elephants or assemble aluminium boats and paddle down rivers.

In the autumn of 1958, we came home to Scotland, flying on a Qantas Super Constellation with its three distinctive tail fins and a kangaroo painted on the upper surface of its wings. Living in Edinburgh was to be my first experience of the mother country. My life in colour was about to switch to black and white.

CHAPTER 3

Edinburgh

My parents had bought a ground floor and basement flat in the west end of Edinburgh in Lansdowne Crescent, near St Mary's Cathedral. My bedroom was at the front of the basement, looking onto a blackened stone wall covered with green moss which flourished in the gentle drizzles that had replaced the sharp tropical downpours of Assam.

May May stayed until Deborah and I started as day pupils at a home school in the Grange district of Edinburgh, the plan being that we would become boarders when my parents were next posted out east. I should remember the moment of our parting because she had looked after me every day of my life, but I do not.

During the holidays a home school becomes a home for those children unable to return to their real homes, usually because their parents lived abroad. It was a remnant of empire that survived with a diminishing demand.

Deborah and I were taken to a school outfitter to be equipped with our uniform of, in my case, grey woollen shorts and a lovat green jumper, covering scratchy woollen underwear. For formal occasions I had a kilt with a bodice attached, as my body had not yet developed hips on which a kilt might hang. For outdoor wear, I had a beige wool coat with a dark brown velvet collar of a type now worn only by royal children or children of those who aspire to be royal. On my head I wore a beige tam o'shanter with a blue pompom which I was taught to take off when entering a building or when a hearse passed by.

Deborah and Neil at the Botanical Gardens,
Edinburgh in Spring 1959

If I missed the colours and the heat of Assam, I do not recall it, though my life changed from an outdoor one to an indoor one. I was entranced as I watched from the drawing room the horse that pulled the milk cart standing in the street, its breath condensing as it munched the contents of its nose bag, while the milkman darted backwards and forwards delivering his orders.

Later, if he was driving us to school, Norman would go out with a jug of tepid water to melt the ice that had formed overnight on the windscreen of our Hillman Minx. Once we were on the move, he would rub the inside of the glass with a chamois leather to remove the condensation until eventually the heater produced a cuticle of clear glass through which he could see by crouching low in his seat.

The car had no flashing indicator lights but instead had illuminated orange electro-mechanical arms that were designed to spring up from the door pillars like prosthetic fingers pointing our intended way, though in practice they were often shy about breaking cover. If there was even a suspicion of ice, they never came out. In addition to being unreliable, the 'dickies', as they were called, were largely invisible from most directions. As a result, whenever we crossed large intersections where policemen were directing traffic on point duty, Norman would press the palm of his left hand against the windscreen to indicate that we were going straight ahead or would wind down the driver's window, introducing a cold blast, to give the hand signal for a turn.

It was my first experience of living as a family on our own without servants and the first time I had seen a kitchen. It became the room we lived in most. Nothing was fitted. By the window was a deep ceramic sink and draining board. On the wall to the right was a gas cooker on elegantly slender legs, its skeleton of exposed steel exuding an industrial strength. To the left, was a white enamelled fridge, also on long legs. In between were free-standing units for storage. I would often sit, drawing or playing with toys at a table in an alcove, while Nancie went about the housework to the tune of 'Music While You Work', a programme of light orchestral music broadcast by the BBC to sugar the pill of industry.

Norman had bought the valve radio on hire-purchase but then felt so badly that he had used credit to buy something he should have saved up for, that he paid off the outstanding balance immediately. The set did not bring the happiness expected, as Nancie had wanted a transistor radio that she could move easily around the house. The fact that its valves gave off the heat of a small radiator was no consolation, even in winter.

Nancie had almost no experience of cooking and so we ate a great deal of baked beans on toast, or possibly that is all I remember because it is what I enjoyed the most. On Sundays after church at Palmerston Place, we had a chicken or a joint of meat, which we ate formally in the dining room. The best part of the meal was at the end when we were given squares of bread that had been dropped onto the carving plate to absorb the intense flavours of the concentrated, salty juices.

Monday was wash day; a day in which the kitchen was converted into a washhouse, with Nancie carrying out the hot, heavy work. Although we owned a washing machine, it was only a twin-tub, that had to be dragged out of its hiding place and wheeled up to the kitchen sink where the machine's drain hose was hooked over the side. Another hose about four feet long was attached to the cold tap of the kitchen sink and its free end poked into the machine whenever water was needed.

The washing process was like dancing a Scottish reel, with only brief moments of inactivity, none of which could be fully enjoyed because of the concentration required to pick up the cue for what to do next. Hoses had to be directed, taps turned on and off, the floor mopped after the hose had slipped out, clothes put in, timers set, scalding hot clothes transferred to the spin drier using wooden tongs, the spin drier filled with water and then set off, the spin drier reloaded when it banged and wouldn't spin because it was out of balance, more spilled water mopped up, the spun clothes removed – everything had to be monitored and an action was needed at every stage. It was not even possible to rest during the washing phase because even the longest timing was a mere four minutes. Dirt must have been crouching on its marks, eager to be released.

The water was never changed and darkened as the morning drew on. When, finally, the last wash was over and the overhead pulley was heavy with clothes, the by now filthy water was drained out of the main tub and Nancie turned to the task of washing and rinsing the woollen items by hand at the sink. By the afternoon the kitchen was warm with steam and fragrant with the perfume of washing powder – and Nancie was exhausted. The task of ironing the following day seemed almost like fun.

In early 1959, Norman took up a post in Bangladesh. Before he left, Deborah and I began to take the bus to school, starting under his guidance and later doing the journey on our own. As a child, the etiquette for behaviour on a bus was simple and I knew that I only had a right to sit down if every adult was seated.

In May of 1959 Nancie joined Norman in Bangladesh and Deborah and I became weekly boarders at the school.

My parents' intention was that we stay at school through the summer holidays until Christmas, when they were due to return home on leave, though events were to change that plan. The moment of parting on the school steps was hard as I hugged Nancie tightly before watching her drive off. I was five years old. Many years later, I learned that my tears had dried long before hers. Nature does not reward mothers who abandon their offspring, however noble their intentions.

The family photograph that was taken just before Deborah and Neil went to boarding school for the first time in Spring 1959.

The school building was an Edinburgh mansion. Though brutalised for institutional use with hard surfaces and conduit piping, its proportions and detailing were the vocabulary and good manners of a gentleman down on his luck.

The house was set in substantial grounds, a third of which was given over to vegetables, the surviving patch in a garden once entirely dug for victory. We were free to ride round the paths on our bikes, boneshakers with solid tyres that took effort to propel. At the front of the house, we climbed the pine trees, making our way as close as we dared to the top. No one gave us permission but, in our world, everything was allowed unless it was expressly forbidden.

Lessons at elementary school are like booster rockets that fall away largely unremembered, apart from the joyful production of tat at Christmas.

Our reading primer was about a farmer called Old Lob. He came back to haunt me some fifty-five years later as I was interviewing Nancie at BBC Scotland as part of a project to record people's lives. We had talked for twice the allotted time, and I was trying to bring the interview to an end. As recommended by the BBC, I asked Nancie in a concluding question if, as she looked back on her life, she had any regrets. She thought for a moment and then in an answer of political brilliance, said she wished I'd been taught to read properly. I never understood her anxiety, as I have never had the slightest difficulty in reading.

When we were not having lessons, we were free to play or were taken for long walks on paths that ran up steeply between the gorse bushes of nearby Blackford Hill. There were no organised games. In the afternoon, we had a compulsory rest when we lay down on blankets spread out on the brown linoleum of the classroom floor. Children were expected to have a fallow period.

In addition to instructing us in the three Rs, the school drilled good table manners into us. Naturally, we had to hold our knives and forks properly, eating with our mouths closed and keeping our elbows in, but we were also expected to maintain a radar sweep to check on the needs of others round the table. Older children, particularly the girls, used to stare ostentatiously at their watches as they timed how long we had ignored their needs.

Our good manners did not extend to foreigners. When three children from an American family were temporarily billeted with us, we mocked them not just for their accents but for saying things in a way that was unfamiliar to us. Their refusal to see that they were wrong only made it worse. Our ridicule peaked when one of them complained after going for a walk that she had a rock in her shoe. How we laughed! The very idea! Imagine! A rock! How on earth could there possibly be room for a rock! A stone was quite another matter. There was always room for a stone.

A Kenyan boy called Henry came to the school for a single term. He was the only person in any of my schools – or indeed in my university class – who was not white. I say that purely as an observation and not in any way because I yearn for the days of racial homogeneity.

We accepted Henry more readily than we did the Americans because his English was the same as ours and his foreignness seemed less extreme. After a few weeks, someone told us not to tease him about his curly hair and the special comb and ointment he used on it, and after that we teased him about all three.

During the week, I slept in a dormitory with five other children. They were probably all boys, but I have a feeling that girls and boys were mixed freely both at bath time and at bedtime. The memory of war was still recent, and people's sensibilities were tuned to a coarse setting.

Our physical well-being was the responsibility of Matron, a stout woman with the round, smiling face of a Hollywood Reverend Mother and the steel of a real one. She had two remedies for illness. One was to offer a tumbler of Lucozade, a drink sold under the strapline that it 'aided recovery' though it consisted of little more than glucose and orange-flavoured carbonated water. So full of sugar was it, that it was surprising it still poured. We naturally found it delicious and looked in hope at the bottles on Matron's dispensing shelf, wrapped promisingly in translucent orange plastic film. Her alternative remedy was to paint our tonsils with iodine, using what looked like the largest possible size of artist's brush. Both treatments were expected to cure a wide range of illness and were dispensed randomly, with the result that confessing to feeling unwell held an element of risk.

At the weekends, Deborah and I would go to stay with my paternal grandparents who had by now retired to Balerno, a village then of torpid tranquillity, west of Edinburgh.

We travelled out with Douglas on a green country bus service. On the journey we always insisted on sitting on the back seat of the upper deck, a place chosen so that every imperfection in the road would fling us into the air. It would be difficult to imagine any activity less likely to appeal to a man in his eighties, but Douglas chuckled indulgently and sometimes joked about paying extra for the bumps.

Within the village, my grandparents lived a life of impeccable respectability in a white, pebbledash bungalow, small enough even for a child to remember it as cramped, but with a large garden. Their road was a place where nothing happened, apart from the arrival of various vans that, at the sound of a horn, sold provisions to ensure that no one need risk the excitement of the high street, some of whose shops were occasionally open. Even the street name, 'Lovedale Road', suggested a sterile harmony dreamt up in the office of a speculative builder in the aftermath of the Great War. Only the sound of rain dripping from the gutters and the occasional horn disturbed the silence.

Lizzie, ever the genteel Edinburgh woman, was always careful to put on a hat when she went out of the house, even if only going to buy something from one of the vans in the road. Before her marriage, she had taken a six-month cookery course designed to help young ladies manage their households. Over the years, as a minister's wife on a meagre income, she had used the skills she had learned to make meals using cheap ingredients. On a Friday afternoon, she would have 'a spread' waiting for us – a high tea with homemade scones, cakes and possibly a cheese soufflé. There was not a vegetable in sight.

Ten weeks after Nancie had said goodbye on the school steps, my parents received a letter from the headmistress, saying that Deborah had a puffy face and at the doctor's recommendation was in the Sick Children's Hospital. She had thoughtfully added that there was nothing to worry about, thus putting my parents into a state of immediate alarm.

They consulted the company doctor who suggested that Nancie should return from Bangladesh to Edinburgh immediately. The advice was sound. Shortly after she arrived back, Deborah was diagnosed with kidney lupus, a disease for which there was no cure, and which, it was predicted, would shortly end her life.

The centre of kidney transplant expertise was in Boston, Massachusetts and over the next year, the consultant treating Deborah would fly across for meetings, bringing with him an increasingly large file of her case notes. Had Deborah had an identical twin, they might have risked a transplant, but they feared that even a kidney from me would have been rejected.

After her meetings with the hospital doctors, Nancie would book a phone call to pass the news on to Norman. At a cost of five pounds – a week's wages for a working man – they would speak for three minutes.

I knew the calls were important although I had no appreciation why. In our house, as in many at the time, our black Bakelite telephone was kept on a table in the hall where it would be equally inconvenient to reach from any room in the house.

In the minutes before the call had been booked to start, Nancie would go into the hall and stand by the phone, coiled as a spring, reading and re-reading her notes. Then the phone would ring, and the operator would ask if she would take the call.

It is not easy to communicate complex information in a short time. Air traffic controllers can do it, but they and the pilots with whom they speak use a limited vocabulary and have set phrases with precise meanings. For two people using the verbose language of lay people to describe a disease and treatment that they were only beginning to understand – and to do it in three minutes – was an impossible task.

The calls began with desperate expressions of love, blurted out in tears and they ended when the operator, with detached inhumanity, came on the line to say the three minutes were up. In between, Nancie did her best to cover the points she had written in her notes. There was never enough time to tell of other matters such as the incident on the bus when a woman had observed loudly that Deborah, by now inflated by cortisone, was a very fat little girl. At the end of the three short minutes, they were dragged apart and left to pour out their feelings in typed air letters. Far from feeling resentful, they regarded the chance to talk as miraculous.

The year between diagnosis of Deborah's disease and her death was Nancie's Calvary, her pride at her daughter's courage only increasing the agony of the prospect of her loss.

The evening Deborah died, Alasdair and I were watching a television drama about men in helicopters fighting fires in California. In the middle of the programme, an ambulance drew up in the street outside our house and two uniformed men appeared with a stretcher. The doctor was in Deborah's bedroom and broke the news to her that she was going back into hospital. I heard her say, 'Oh, no!' It was the last time I heard her voice. My parents both went with her, Norman having returned from Bangladesh two days earlier.

The following morning, four of us were sitting round the dining room table having breakfast. No one spoke until I did.

I had been growing flowers in the garden and asked if I could take them to Deborah. Nancie cried and said that wouldn't be possible. I persisted, Nancie said she had gone to God. Having no idea what that meant, I kept asking 'why not' in the whine that children adopt when refused the answer they want to hear. Eventually, Nancie said that Deborah had died, spitting out the words in a hoarse whisper. That was when I cried.

I learned later that the last words Deborah had said were 'water, water' when she was in the ambulance. At the hospital, my parents were ushered from her bedside at the very moment of her death, a betrayal that haunted Nancie for the rest of her life. Worse was to come for Norman who was unfortunate enough to find an undertaker devoid of compassion. The man treated his task as if it were the disposal of a lump of meat, leaving Norman sick to the core.

We took a short holiday in a village in Fife, staying in a cottage that had been lent to us by a friend who was the Bishop of Edinburgh. The house was a simple 'but and ben' construction. Much of the furniture was covered with wallpaper to make it appear fresh and modern. Thin curtains hung on stretched wires to create a hidden space in which to hang clothes. There was no bathroom and we washed at the kitchen sink. It was far removed from our usual life and broke our normal rhythms. Nancie took an easel to the edge of a cornfield and in her grief painted the view of the village with the kirk set up on the high ground. While Nancie painted, Norman took Alasdair and me to hack round the links golf course at Elie and go for long walks.

For my parents, the pain of Deborah's death would never ease. The very mention of her name would forever make Nancie cry, but I had the protection of a sibling. As naturally as healing a cut, I amputated all memory of her apart from the circumstances of her death, and was freed to live my life, unburdened by sorrow. As a family we re-formed, and I edged up as wingman to Alasdair to become a team of two.

I returned to the home school for the start of the winter term, having just had my seventh birthday. Someone asked me what I had done in the holidays and I replied that my sister had died. I had become proud of that statement, having discovered that it gave me power over other people and made them treat me with special kindness. Matron, who had overheard the exchange, told me there was no need to talk about it.

Alasdair and Neil in Karachi 1961

Shortly before Christmas, I received a letter saying that Alasdair and I would now be going to Karachi, Norman having been transferred to work there. The headmistress showed me on a globe where the city was, pointing out helpfully that I would be swimming in the Indian Ocean.

I flew down to London on a BEA Viscount, wearing my kilt. It was the first time I had flown by myself. As a very young person travelling on my own, I was referred to as a VYP and given a badge with silver and red diagonals on it which indicated that I needed shepherding. In later years, children on their own were referred to as UMs, an acronym that more perfectly captures the cluelessness of the unaccompanied minor.

As the Viscount approached London and prepared to land, my feelings of anxiety turned to horror when the wing appeared to be breaking off at the trailing end. I wondered if anyone else had noticed but was too afraid to say anything.

At Heathrow Airport, I was met by my uncle and aunt who took me in their yellow Austin A40 van to their house in Cheam where Alasdair joined me from his prep school in Hampshire.

We spent the night sleeping head to toe in a single bed with a thick eiderdown on it. In the corner of the room, a gas fire hissed, glowing warmly, until my aunt switched it off as she went to bed. By the morning, ice had formed on the inside of the windowpanes.

The following evening, we returned to Heathrow where we said farewell to my uncle before following the trail of brown lights that guided us to the part of the apron where the BOAC Comet 4C was lit up, precious under arc lights.

The aircraft was breathtakingly beautiful. The white

painted roof, the blue swish line below it and the Speedbird on the tail suggested power and strength. Not just any power and strength, but British power and strength. In case anyone needed reminding, there was a discreet Union flag on the tail fin.

Everyone boarded by the steps at the rear port side. I was not aware of it at the time but inside there was a hierarchy of luxury, though the terms 'First Class' and 'Deluxe' made it clear that no one should expect neglect.

The take-off was dramatic but so advanced was the Comet that it was neither more nor less exciting than that of a modern aeroplane. My parents, used to slower, propeller driven aircraft, marvelled at the thrust and the rate of climb and talked of 'going upstairs', but with the insouciance of a young person, I accepted the experience as normal and merely found it exciting.

We landed at Rome in the middle of the night to refuel. Inevitably there was a 'technical hitch', a term we came to know well. If there is one major difference between the Comet and its worker ant descendants, it is that the Comet required to be repaired every time it touched the ground. Passengers were resigned to it, even expecting it.

After Rome came Beirut, where we arrived in the heat of the day. I missed hearing the pilot's warning that the runway was short, and that thrust reversal would be applied on landing. As a result, I was unprepared for the violence of the experience which I found even more terrifying than the apparent disintegration of the Viscount's wing on the flight from Edinburgh. I thought it was the end of everything. Alasdair said that in future I should listen more carefully to what I was being told.

We taxied to the terminal where a guard of honour had lined up on the apron. A red carpet was then unrolled, allowing a figure in flowing white robes to be greeted respectfully as he descended from the rear door. It was not a courtesy extended to those of us merely flying Deluxe.

I had not yet understood perspective and when the Comet had been on final approach to land, I had become very excited by the model cars that I had seen below us. I tried to speak to Alasdair about it, but he thought I was being deliberately obtuse and refused to engage. He must have been tired.

In the late afternoon, we landed at Karachi and walked out of the cool of the aircraft into a wall of heat, screwing up my eyes against the glare of the sun. Hot air tore at my lungs and I whimpered that I couldn't breathe. Fortunately, I soon acclimatised.

To live in the East was to be pampered in a comfortable cocoon of success and vigour. The ex-patriate British community was a society of those in the prime of life. There were no old people who needed to be visited on a Sunday afternoon for dull conversations over high tea. Everyone was a Kennedy – young, energetic, handsome and rich enough for their absolute wealth not to matter.

I never knew the nature of Norman's work for the Burmah Oil Company. Even adults struggle to describe the work done by their spouse or child, and as a child I had neither understanding nor interest. All I knew was that he must be important because we lived in a large house that had once housed a sultan's harem and had a turret. We also had eight servants. I used to count them in my head, just as boys at school used to count the number of rooms in their houses. The exercise was not as simple as it sounds. In the same way that it could be hard to argue that a large scullery or small dressing room counted as a room, so it was that there were borderline judgements to be made about whether certain people counted as servants. To reach my figure of eight, I had to give myself the benefit of the doubt.

Without question, our three bearers could be included. Always smartly turned out in white uniforms and red turbans, they served us at mealtimes, made our beds and lived in the servants' quarters in the compound.

33 Clifton, Karachi

Cook too was an obvious inclusion, though he was an unseen figure because the kitchen was an unexplored place. I would often hear Nancie talking heatedly with him in the dining room as she tried to keep his fraud within accepted limits, but I found the confrontation disturbing and avoided it. If I ever saw cook, I do not remember it.

Baboo, our driver, was an ex-military man and was intensely proud of having fought for the British. He wore his uniform and medals every day, his chest pushed out in pride. He was scrupulous in his adherence to the professional drivers' code which required that the more important a passenger, the closer to the crown of the road he should be driven. Fortunately, the code permitted a face-saving bacon-slice if two important people were travelling in opposite directions. Baboo was a good friend to me and made me catapults, so his place on the list was assured.

The mali tended the garden, which consisted of parched grass and geraniums grown in pots, and the durwan guarded the house at night. Their claim for inclusion was strong because they worked exclusively for us, even though they did not live in the servants' quarters.

The dhobi wallah was a borderline case because he came in to do the laundry, a task he performed at the back of the house on a concrete slab. He would squat on his haunches as he bashed the laundry on stones before twisting it mercilessly and hanging it out on the line to dry. He very probably worked for other households too, but I claimed him because he was around so often. My compromise was not to count the sweepers and other cleaners who were always drifting in and around the house.

In the midst of the gentle buzz of the household at 33 Clifton, I led a solitary life. In the mornings I was taught at home by Nancie in a turret room set apart for the purpose.

I can recall nothing of those lessons apart from her tip that I would recall how to spell the word 'hear' if I remembered that I 'hear' things with my 'ear'.

I had a friend called Sandy who lived nearby and who quite often 'came to play', but for much of the day I was left on my own. To amuse myself, I would play records on the radiogram in the sitting room. Ignoring the classical and band music in my parents' collection, I played Flanders and Swann, *Anna Russell Sings Again* and *The Best of Sellers* until I became so familiar with them that I absorbed the words and the comic timing without knowing why the audience was laughing. That understanding came over the years, each revelation a piece of the jigsaw.

At the start of 1961, I was given a kitten named Lilibet in honour of the Queen who was due to come out for an official visit to Pakistan the following month. Shortly after Lilibet arrived, she nearly left again when a black kite swooped down on her while she was in the garden and grabbed her with his talons. Fortunately, she slipped free and fell safely to the ground.

The real Lilibet had a more successful trip. I waved a Union flag by the side of the street while she drove past standing up in an open car, unprotected from assassin or the sun. In the evening, my parents went off excitedly to the formal reception at the State Guest House, Nancie's dress rustling as she came into my bedroom to give me a scented kiss before leaving.

Shortly after they had gone, a rainstorm of terrible intensity hit the city. Almost immediately leaks appeared in the roof of our house and the servants rushed round with buckets trying to place them under the worst of

Lilibet

the flows. The following day I learned that a tented area at the royal reception had collapsed under the weight of rainwater and the guests had been soaked. Fortunately, the Queen had pretended that the dispirited people presented to her were still in mint condition. Everyone thought she had been absolutely marvellous. One can go a long way with good manners.

The Queen was also widely praised for her discipline in keeping to her schedule, in contrast to Jacqueline Kennedy who, a year later, was reputed to have let her schedule slip to pursue interests of her own. No one said that Americans had no idea how to behave but everyone thought it.

The first film I ever saw was *Around the World in 80 Days*. The cinema was of simple construction and I could see daylight under the seats where the sun crept in under the scaffolding. The film was not enjoyable. Even though I was seven, I was naïve enough to believe it was a record of real events that had been filmed by someone with a cine camera who just happened to be at the scene. As Shirley MacLaine was about to be immolated on the funeral pyre of her late husband in a scene so artificial that it now seems risible, I was so frightened I could scarcely breathe. When Phileas Fogg was being attacked with arrows by Native Americans as he went through the desert in a train, I was petrified. On the way home, all the adults were laughing as if it had been a jolly romp. I was still trembling. It had been a very close-run thing.

On Sundays we went to the Anglican church for the morning service. Nancie, still raw from Deborah's death, would break down when singing and to my horror would keep going, her voice choking as she wept. It was as embarrassing as when she broke the golden rule never to attempt a descant from the pews.

Apart from the requirement to go to church, I looked forward to Sundays because in the late morning, Baboo would drive us to Balaji Beach where the Burmah Oil Company had a concrete beach house with a covered veranda. I was always anxious about the drive there because we had to go at slow speed along a rutted track through a refugee camp. As soon as they saw us, small boys would gather round the doors banging on the window and shouting 'baksheesh' as they begged for money. I wanted to open the car doors and shake the beggars off, but Nancie would put an arm round me and calm me down.

Alasdair, Nancie and Neil in Karachi 1961

Once we had arrived, we would sit in the shade on upholstered rattan furniture, drinking cool drinks from the lead-lined icebox, while Baboo disappeared into the house with his paraffin cooker to heat up lunch. The sand was too hot to walk on in bare feet, so we would have to put on flipflops to go to the ocean, where we would swim in the huge waves that lifted us up and down. Nancie was careful to limit the amount of time I spent in the sun and covered me in protective cream but even so, after four months, for the first and only time in my life, I had a coffee and vanilla tan.

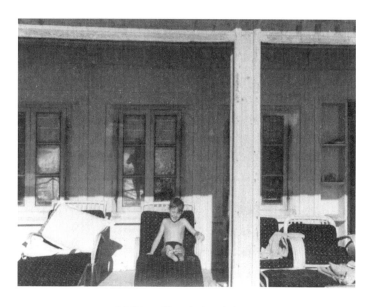

Neil in a Karachi beach house.

In May 1961, I joined Alasdair at a prep school in Winchester where, unusually, I had been allowed to start in the summer rather than the autumn term.

On the evening before we were due to leave Karachi, the two of us lay together in the bath, arranged in our established order of precedence; he at the sloping end and I at the tap end. The room was warm after the fierce air-conditioning of our bedroom and the yellow light of the late afternoon sun slipped through the blue-grey shutters, painting the walls with stripes. As I slopped water gently over my chest, he briefed me on how to behave at school.

With the wisdom of an eleven-year-old, he started with the matter that would be most pressingly important. I needed to change the way I referred to my private parts. Up to that point, I had used childish names that had developed within the family for reasons forgotten, but Alasdair told me that these words had to be left behind. From now on I would have a P and a B. I would also have balls; the word being allowed in full to avoid ambiguity with my B.

Continuing his briefing, he explained how I should relate to him. He was four years older than me and had a desk in the Senior Common Room which I, as a junior, could enter only by invitation for a particular purpose. Ideally, I should avoid all contact with him but if that were not possible, I was on no account to call him Alasdair. He was Swan 1 and I was Swan 2.

As a final assurance, he said that in my first term a boy would be allocated to be my 'substance' and it would be his job to help me, his 'shadow', find my way round.

We went to bed early and were awoken by Nancie in the early hours of the morning to get ready for our flight to London, which was due to leave in the cool before dawn while the air was still dense. Bleary with sleep, we dressed in our kilts.

My parents had two fears when we flew on our own. The first was that someone would give us something to take through customs. This struck me as odd but, as it seemed to worry them a great deal, I always promised faithfully that any request would be refused, though I wondered what I would do if it were chocolate.

Their second concern was that we might go missing at one of the two intermediate refuelling stops, usually Rome or Zurich and Cairo or Beirut. With the 'technical hitches' often resulting in long delays, the possibility of an unaccompanied minor drifting away from the custody of a temporarily distracted BOAC air hostess was not entirely fanciful. Norman had decided that two boys wearing kilts would be easy to describe and easy to spot, a decision that was hard to challenge.

My parents' insistence that I wore a kilt caused me great embarrassment. While I was proud to wear the kilt in Scotland, I was under the misapprehension that it would be regarded as a skirt in any other country, especially in England. I might not have been sure about much, but I knew that wearing girls' clothing was inconsistent with being a boy and I squirmed with self-consciousness.

On the drive to the airport in our Ford Zodiac, Alasdair sat on the front bench seat next to Baboo while I sat in the back between my parents, snuggled up against Nancie. She was close to tears but kept telling me how many new friends I would make, as if she was applying witch-hazel.

Although apprehensive about starting at a new school, I was excited by the prospect of the trip. After my first flight in the Comet at the end of the previous year, I had become immensely proud of her, imitating her take-off on the beach where I ran as fast as I could with my arms outstretched, roaring at the top of my voice. It was the love of one who remained innocently unaware of her darker side.

Over the course of its service, the Comet had crashed or had serious incidents at most of the stops on the route to London. Eight years earlier there had been a fatal crash at Karachi itself. As I was to discover fifty-five years later after carrying out a Google search on the aircraft registration number in my Junior Jet Club logbook, the aircraft I was about to board had been badly damaged at Beirut airport some eighteen months earlier and had been extensively rebuilt.

It is easy to be critical of the Comet now that the design of a modern jet airliner has evolved in a quite different way, but much thought had gone into making her as she was. Unfortunately, the drawbacks of the design proved greater than the advantages and as a commercial proposition, she was a disaster. Just as Concorde a decade later, she was not to be developed and became little more than a kinetic sculpture bought with taxpayers' cash by a government intent on technological development but with a lofty disdain for what the market needed.

But I was innocent of these matters and infatuated with her looks and speed. She fuelled the pride I already had in all things British. Any decent toy had 'Made in England' stamped on it. All our clothes and shoes were made in Britain. The British made the best cars in the world. Our Queen was the most important Queen in the world. The Comet was obviously the most advanced aircraft in the world. Any fool knew that.

After we had landed at Heathrow, we were taken by my aunt and uncle to their house to change into our school uniforms, a celebration of grey, relieved only by the plain green of our ties and caps.

At Waterloo Station we were met by a lugubrious French master called Worm, who put a tick on his list next to our names and invited us to enter one of the three compartments that had been reserved for us in a carriage of the steam train to Southampton.

Having said goodbye to my parents earlier in the day, I was already calmed by distance and watched with detachment through the carriage window as other boys hugged their tearful mothers and shook hands with their fathers.

By now I was suffering from what was later to be called jetlag and remember little of the journey until we reached Winchester.

CHAPTER 4

Winchester

I arrived at prep school in a Rolls Royce Phantom motor car. It was one of two identical vehicles owned by a local taxi firm. The cars were known affectionately as Albert and Ernie, the names being demanded by their registration plates that began ALB and ERN.

As we glided down the hill from Winchester Station to the school in the cathedral close, I saw the redbrick core of the school, designed by Christopher Wren, flanked by the oak framed structure of the Pilgrims' Hall and Priory Stables. The buildings had been worn and bleached by time and weather, eroding artifice and leaving them as natural as the trees that spread their shade on the deanery lawn. It felt a gentle place.

On the first morning I took in the alarming sight of the masters lining up for assembly after breakfast, wearing their academic gowns and mortar boards. Up to that point, the only men I had come across in school had tended the garden or fed the boiler with coke. These men exuded authority. I must have looked daunted because one of them smiled at me reassuringly and said they only dressed like that on the first morning of term. I didn't appreciate it at the time, but the flash of empathy was a sign of my good fortune at my parents' choice of school. By lunchtime, the masters had sloughed off their academic skins and emerged in their softer uniform of tweed and corduroy.

The dormitory I was put in, appropriately called Dorm 1, was an elegantly proportioned room that looked across a lawn to a cedar tree. There were no curtains and the evening light shone through the astragalled panes of the two large sash windows. Round the perimeter of the room were ranged ten narrow, metal-framed beds on the dark wooden floor. Between each bed was a simple wooden chair.

On my first night, when I had been almost asleep at supper, Sister – a trained nurse who had responsibility for our health and discipline in the dormitories – had guided me to my bed near the window and told me how to undress discreetly, explaining that in the process I should always turn to face my chair and never remove my shirt until my P and B were safely contained in whatever clothing I was changing into.

We washed ourselves at a basin with our shorts or pyjama bottoms on, even after sport. Baths were taken twice a week in single bathrooms that had doors that closed. There were no locks on the door but the only person who ever came in was Sister to make sure we had washed properly using one of the ubiquitous cubes of red carbolic soap. When we swam, we wore swimming trunks. Our private parts remained private except when we as boys lifted each other's shirts to shout 'sights!'. At the time it was unremarkable. Now it seems exceptional.

There were fewer than ninety boys at the school, of whom twenty were in the cathedral choir, the remaining seventy being 'Commoners'. In a history of the school, it was recorded that in the 1930s there had been a concern that the Commoners might feel like second-class pupils. If that had been the case, the concern had been addressed by the time I arrived. With extraordinary philistinism we pitied the choir because they were not able to go home at Easter and Christmas. The fact that they received a gold-standard musical education that would give them joy all their lives seemed to us to be little compensation for missing turkey and all the trimmings at home.

The class sizes were small, the largest being twelve and the smallest eight. The classrooms were simple and contained only desks and a blackboard. The desks were traditional in style with seats attached and lids that lifted to reveal a space for books. In the top right-hand corner was an inkwell that was regularly filled by a handyman. Left-handed people would have had a long stretch if they were to dip their pens, but the problem was simply resolved by the instruction that they should write using their right hands.

Writing with a dip-pen resulted in inkblots and ink spillages, immortalised by Ronald Searle in the Molesworth books. In order to absorb the ink, we were issued with pink blotting paper called blotch. It was accepted wisdom that if blotch was soaked in ink and rolled up after it had dried, it would be good to smoke. Support for the theory was established during a carpentry lesson, when we saw our woodwork master light a blotch cigarette from his paraffin stove and smoke it with apparent pleasure.

Masters often smoked in class and tossed the fag-ends casually out of the window, ashtrays not being part of classroom equipment. In imitation, we would sit happily in the school yard on a summer day, using a magnifying glass and the sun's rays to light our own blotch cigarettes, though we only puffed them and dared not inhale. Cigarettes were part of life. We even had sweet cigarettes that we would pretend to smoke luxuriantly.

It is hard to remember anything in detail about most of our lessons, though we were fortunate in having masters who were good at bringing their subjects alive. One told us how to design an aeroplane and instructed us in the principles of flight, a practical series of lessons that I found absorbing. That same man also taught us that adjectives and adverbs were to be used as if they were gold dust. I remember him introducing us to 'Winter Song' by Shakespeare, not just because the boy reading it started 'When icky leas hang from the wall' but from the word picture so economically conjured. The Maths master refused to accept that anyone would 'not get' Maths and made us play around with numbers until they became old friends and we could see how they linked and related. There wasn't a single boy who left the school unconfident in the subject. None of the teachers appeared to be constrained by what they might teach. When I asked one evening after prep how a car turned petrol into motion, the master arranged for a Ford Anglia engine to be brought in for us to strip down and assemble.

The curriculum was very different from a modern one. There was little science, though biology was tentatively introduced at the end of my time, courtesy of Nuffield who paid for it. The master was a Scot who had us running about in the school grounds, setting down one-metre square frames on the lawn and counting the number of leaves the earth worms had pulled down into their holes. He also had a film of a cat eating its food and we had to note how it looked suspiciously over its shoulder in case someone was going to eat either it, or its food. There was no sound to the film and he provided a commentary. When he talked of the 'cut eatin' the fud' we forgot all good manners and howled with laughter. After the lesson was over and he was gone, we mimicked him as we dispersed.

Our French accents were no better than our Scottish ones. Most of us blundered out words with Churchillian insensitivity. One boy, my friend Earwig, had a good accent. His family were most unusual in going abroad for their summer holidays, in their case to France, with their camping kit secured on a roof rack. His mother, being a French teacher, must have helped him too. When he read French aloud, we thought he sounded almost as amusing as the biology master.

In Latin we used the standard Kennedy's Shorter Latin Primer, the words on the cover inked over to read 'Shortbread Eating Primer', and declined nouns, adjectives and pronouns, chanting them out to get the rhythm into our heads. We could never see the point of learning the language, reciting the schoolboy's lament that 'Latin is a language as dead as dead can be. It killed ten thousand Romans and now it's killing me.' We were reassured that it would help us use English accurately. At the time, it felt like an unwanted gift, but now it feels like a treasure.

In Geography we spent a great deal of time with a billiard cue pointing out places on a world map yellowing with age. Countries were largely coloured red which made us appreciate how much of the world we had controlled and still did. When it came to the United Kingdom we pointed at the location of potteries, steel mills, collieries and car manufacturing. We were a great exporting nation. It was possible to feel the continuing pulse of production.

Although there were no beatings in class, the masters could be physical. If they looked over your shoulder and thought what you were writing was particularly dim-witted, they might slap you across the head, or if they thought you were drifting off to sleep they would throw a piece of chalk or even the wooden board eraser in your direction.

On Wednesdays and Saturdays, lessons stopped at lunchtime to enable us to play matches. For away fixtures we would board a coach, but if only a single team was playing, we would sometimes go in the two Rolls Royce Phantom taxis. Nobody cared how many bodies piled in, so there was always room for scorers, umpires and referees.

The ethos of the school was that we should always subordinate our interests to those of others. It was also made explicit that little boys should be seen and not heard. For someone shy like me, it was not the guidance I needed.

Homesickness is a problem that boarding schools like to deny, the very word 'sickness' making it seem that a yearning for one's family is in some way a malady. At our school it was addressed by the simple expedient of limiting the amount of time boys went home. The logic was impeccable; if you are not reminded of how pleasant it is to be at home, you will not hanker to be there. Nancie managed to arrange for the rules, normally so inviolable, to be bent for the last Sunday afternoon of my first term but it did not end well for me.

Alasdair and I spent an afternoon with her and had a picnic in the sun in a park. When the time came to say goodbye, I cried. The following morning during breakfast, the headmaster's wife beckoned me over to her table. I thought she might have something pleasant to say, so I trotted over. The moment she started to speak I knew I had miscalculated. Crying was evidently a serious lapse of good form. Did I understand that by my behaviour, I had let down my brother, my parents, myself and the school? I didn't really but understood the expected answer so looked suitably penitent and tried hard not to aggravate the offence by repeating it. I hadn't brought down the government, but it must have been a close-run thing.

Half-term was meagre, consisting only of a Saturday and a Sunday. Bizarrely, for my first three years, we were required to spend the Saturday night back at school, such was the fear of the softening influence of home.

I was fortunate that my friend Earwig used to invite me to his home. He was known as Earwig because he was so small. His family lived in a terraced house in Old Portsmouth opposite a bomb site. His father worked in London and his mother taught French at Portsmouth Grammar School. They both smoked furiously, laughed easily and enjoyed the social life of their community, popping round to the pub at the end of their street for their five o'clock beer.

Earwig's father would collect usually four of us from school and drive us at speed through the Hampshire villages in his

Austin 1100. We loved the journey and bounced around, unrestrained by seat belts. We were quite unconcerned, as we knew that we could brace ourselves against the dashboard or back seat if we saw we were going to crash.

As soon as we arrived at Earwig's house, we would go down into the basement which had been turned into a domestic pub. There were no windows, the only illumination coming from two low-wattage, raffia-covered bottle lamps and some coloured Christmas lights. Within a few minutes of our arriving, Earwig's mother would bring us cheese straws, hot from the oven, and a bottle of sweet cider. Soon we were happily intoxicated as we lifted the lid of the Dansette record player to stack the familiar 45rpm records on the spindle.

Earwig's house, Old Portsmouth

The recordings were of innocent songs, many of them pedalling optimistic messages about the goodness inherent in people. In 'Little White Bull' by Tommy Steele, the white bull turned out to be the equal of the black bulls, an encouraging message of racial harmony. 'My Old Man's a Dustman' reassured us that even the meanest of workmen could have a flashing intellect. 'Ugly Duckling' was all about knowing who you were. The one song without an uplifting message was 'Yellow Polka Dot Bikini' which told of the angst felt by a young woman when she first went to the beach with most of her flesh on show. To begin with she didn't dare come out of the changing room without the protection of a blanket which curiously enough was provided to her. When she managed to overcome her inhibition sufficiently to slide decorously into the water, she didn't dare come out and got cold. In every sense she was a woman completely out of her depth, and we thought she was rather silly, a judgement I now think was too kind.

We knew the lyrics of these few songs by heart yet we never tired of them. There was reassurance in their familiarity because they were often played on the BBC Light Programme. Besides, there were no other records.

During lunch, the alcohol continued to flow, with Earwig's parents drinking wine and the rest of us drinking sweet sherry. Everything seemed funny and we roared with laughter. It was quite unlike the Sunday lunches we used to have with my grandparents when conversation was predictably pleasant, and alcohol remained in the sherry bottle.

When the rules were changed to allow us to spend one night of half-term away from school, I discovered that

Earwig's house had the unimaginable luxury of unlimited hot water for the bath. The source was a geyser gas hot water system, contained in a white cylinder fixed to the wall over the tap end. At the base of the cylinder was a black knurled knob and from the bottom protruded a thin chromed pipe. When you turned the knob there was a roar as the gas ignited and a slow trickle of scalding water came out of the pipe.

While the flow of water was meagre, the endlessness of supply was revolutionary, at once removing the need for diplomatic negotiations before taking a bath and the ever-present threat of a tepid bath. If you had a free half-hour, you could have a deep, hot bath. It was joyous.

I grew to know and love Earwig's family, who were unfailingly good to me during my time at school, and their relaxed hedonism was a strong influence on my own life.

My parents knew only that Earwig's family looked after me and were blissfully unaware that we drank alcohol and rode round Portsmouth on our bicycles in what must have been a semi-intoxicated state. Their ignorance is hardly surprising as the only communication they had from me was a weekly letter which I believed had to follow a standard style that was written on a blackboard by the headmaster. It always began with sporting news: 'Last week the First XI played West Downs away and lost 1 – 2.' Then it might continue with 'On Friday Miss Brewis gave a talk with slides on Portugal.'

Miss Brewis was a woman who we thought must be in her sixties, who used to give lectures once or twice a year on her travels in continental Europe. The Iberian peninsula was her favourite area and the Moorish invasion her favourite theme. The Moors sounded jolly unpleasant because they came uninvited in hoards and did jolly bad things, though they left behind some jolly decent buildings and mosaics.

The great attraction of Miss Brewis's lectures were her slides, not just because of the comedic value of a certain number of them being shown upside down or back to front, or even because the master in charge of the projector sometimes missed the bang of the billiard cue on the floor, requiring her to shout 'Next!' in a stern voice that made us giggle. What really appealed was the vividness of the colour and the sharpness of the images. Colour was a novelty and we rarely saw it reproduced outside the covers of the National Geographic magazines that we pored over.

If there had been other significant events such as a special service in the cathedral, that might be mentioned, but the heart of the correspondence was the report on one's progress.

'Last week my positions in class were:

    Lat
    Maths
    French
    Geog
    Hist
    Script'

After we had copied down the letter, we were meant to wait until the headmaster read out our positions for the week so that we could write them in. Whether it was because I was reluctant to reveal my position in class or because I was careless, I have no recollection, but my parents rarely received a letter from me with the blanks filled in. Thus it was that an air letter from me would be delivered every week to a post box address in Karachi with no news in it of the slightest interest beyond the reassurance that I must have been alive to have written it.

During the week, I occasionally wrote to my grandparents. I enjoyed this type of letter writing because I felt unconstrained by the house style. I liked the ritual of taking out the grey plastic writing case that contained the envelopes, the book of stamps and the pad with its lined sheet that you slipped under the top page to guide your writing. There were no First or Second Class stamps. It was an egalitarian time when all letters were expected to be delivered the day after posting. There were no postcodes, and addresses were easily committed to memory.

My grandmother, Lizzie, was in the habit of forwarding correspondence she had received from one family member to another, so as to keep everyone informed of family news. When eventually one of the letters I had written to her reached Nancie, she cried. The next time she saw me, she asked why I had not felt able to tell her that from my bed I could see the moon rising over the cedar tree and hear the hoot of an owl. I had to tell her it was not what was written on the board. It was only long after I had left the school that I realised that the official style contained only what was considered to be a minimum content.

Letters received for boys were laid out on a small mahogany table. A letter from my parents was a highlight. To this day, no present, however well-chosen, will ever bring the joy I felt on seeing their familiar handwriting on a plump envelope with the word 'Master' in front of my name. Letters from my parents were usually typed so that they would be easy to read. They wrote once a week and burst straight into the news as if years of writing within the constrained space of air letters had disciplined them to avoid clichéd padding. They could not hug or kiss me, nor could they listen to what had happened during my day as we ate supper together, but they could write. While my letters gave them little information to work on, they had another source. Quite unknown to me, the headmaster's wife used to write to my parents about me every week, so they knew much better than I realised how I was doing.

Posting a letter was not without hazard. The headmaster once asked for a volunteer to post a letter for him. A forest of hands went up with boys shouting, 'Sir, sir! Please sir!' Alasdair was chosen, and the letter was handed to him. At this point he made the fatal mistake of looking at the envelope to read the address This was deemed to be impertinence and he was beaten, not harshly, but beaten all the same.

Being beaten was not uncommon. Usually it was for talking after lights out or ragging in the dormitory, an expression which covered anything from fighting to bouncing on the bed. The punishment was always carried out by the headmaster, his weapon of choice being a butter pat or a gym shoe, both of which had a generous surface area which ensured no harm was done.

Sister was a strong influence in our lives. A divorcee in her late thirties, she loved her job and like a good mother, conveyed affection without compromising authority. We enjoyed the cut and thrust of banter with her and she would tousle our hair and send us off when she had had enough. Every night she would open the cupboard in her office that was a dispensary for all the medicines that parents believed would give their sons an extra lustre. I had Minadex, which was a thin liquid filled with vitamins, administered with a teaspoon. To my envy, Earwig and others had Radio Malt, an unctuous substance with the consistency of honey that wound itself deliciously round the soupspoon used to dispense it. It had vitamins too but with the bonus of sugar in large quantity.

Apart from what was in the medicine cabinet, there was little sugar in our diet, and I remember only one boy being overweight. We were unkind to him and teased him by grabbing his spare tyre. I fear he left the school because he was unhappy. The pack was cruel to those who did not fit in. The poor boy must have had some medical condition because it would have been hard to put on weight with what we were fed.

School meals reflected the diet of the times, which was austere, tasteless and dull. The exception was breakfast, when we had fried bread with egg, bacon or tomatoes in rotation. Sadly, to get to the fried bread and its adornment of the day, we had to eat our way through porridge. Served with lumps, it was revolting, becoming the more so as it grew cold and began to set hard. My best friend and I hated it. As we were not allowed to move on to the next course or leave the table until we had finished what was on our plate, he and I were left as two lonely figures in the dining room, swallowing and re-swallowing the porridge until we had eaten sufficient to pass off what remained as being no more than a dirty plate. To our great relief, we had cornflakes in the summer.

Lunch was the largest meal of the day and usually consisted of meat with two vegetables. The meat I dreaded most was mince. Unlike its successor, spag Bol, which is cooked for at least three hours and preferably longer, mince was scarcely cooked at all and was boiled with a little water. The result was tough, gristly and unpalatable.

If mince was undercooked, joints of meat were cooked to the point of ossification before being sawn into discs and rehydrated with gravy made from powdered granules, any 'jus' long having evaporated. Poultry was given similar treatment. Why this was done is a mystery. Possibly it was regarded as safe; bugs would be killed, and no one would complain about seeing blood. Another possible explanation is that cooks followed a formula that specified the cooking time as a number of minutes per pound of weight with a standard time over. As the relationship between the weight of meat and cooking time is not linear, this approach guaranteed that large joints would be overcooked. A cook with curiosity might have thought of shaving a day or so off the cooking time to see what might happen but such a revolution was still some way off. Possibly people liked their meat tough.

If meat was destroyed in the cooking process, so too were vegetables, which were drowned in water and cooked to pulp, but in the 1960s that kind of culinary abuse was considered normal. Even in restaurants, people were not expected to complain if vegetables had been boiling away from the start of the shift until the end of service.

Puddings were prepared with more confidence, and we had the usual range of Dead Man's Leg, Frogspawn and Spotted Dick so beloved by men of middle age in pinstriped suits who know with absolute certainty where those same puddings are still served in City pubs.

High tea consisted typically of pilchards, corned beef or baked beans which would be served on toast. This was followed by sliced white bread and butter on which you could spread a pink jam-like substance. Having our own individual jar of jam, made from fruit and supplied by our parents at the beginning of term, was one of the few ways we were allowed to supplement our diet. The other was by paying for 'extra fruit' which was delivered in a brown paper bag once a week.

The diet, wretched though it was, was healthy and there was little sickness, though some of us feigned it from time to time to avoid a test, a ruse that will have been obvious. Having taken your temperature to make sure you were really as well as you looked, Sister would usually put you back into circulation immediately. If your acting was sufficiently good to raise doubt, she would put you to bed and give you only beef tea to drink and nothing to eat, on the grounds that if you were ill you would have no appetite. By late afternoon you would be feeling very much better.

Every few years there was an epidemic of mumps, measles or chickenpox. Once we had all three together and dormitories had to be converted to sick bays, one for each of the different afflictions. The groans from the measles ward were alarming. Sister reassured us by telling us with a broad smile that the boys in it thought they were dying.

I had mumps and was in rather a jolly ward because, apart from a swollen face, the symptoms were minimal. Earwig was in the bed next to me and asked his younger sister to see if she could get us Mick Jagger's signature after a Rolling Stones concert in Portsmouth. With extraordinary determination, the nine-year-old girl managed to gain access to his dressing room and put forward the request. Much to his credit, Jagger told her to f--- off.

It is painful to watch old television recordings of prep school boys of my era and hear the precious way we used to talk. We now make fun of the Queen when we hear her as a girl inviting Margaret to say good night to the children of empire, but that was our accent.

Our vocabulary seems just as archaic. We said 'Jolly dee' as an expression of approbation. If, like Jagger, we wanted to tell someone to go away, we would say 'Snubs utterly'. The headmaster often referred to things as 'spiffing'. Some of the boys had a precocious vocabulary that had not settled down into plain English and went far beyond the outer limits of style. A boy whom Sister upbraided for playing with a tennis ball in the corridor outside the dormitories replied that his tennis sphere had slipped, and he was endeavouring to arrest it.

School had its own vocabulary. Some of it was borrowed from Winchester College: a 'waggapaga' for wastepaper basket. 'Toyes' were cubicles, similar to those used to define workstations in open plan offices, that senior boys were allowed to make personal with posters and curtains. Other words like 'vacancy' to describe a lavatory had evolved through a process. Every morning immediately after breakfast and before physical training, we were required to evacuate our bowels or at least make an attempt to do so. The duty master of the day kept a list and ticked off people's names as they went off to the toilet block. On their return they had to report how many vacancies there were in the row of toilets so that the right number of boys with bowels not yet evacuated could be detailed off. As a result of this daily use, the word 'vacancy' threw 'toilet' out of the nest and took over.

Recording the evacuation of the bowels of a healthy population of boys was not the only custom that now seems unnecessary. It was also thought important to check that each boy had two testicles. During our time at school we had to go into Sister's room where she and the headmaster's wife would sit either side of the school doctor, like judges in a superior court. Once in the dock, we would drop our shorts and pants while the doctor, a fat man with his stomach held in by a waistcoat, did what was thought necessary.

Sport was played on grounds bounded by the flint walls of the city on three sides and the Bishop's Palace on the fourth.

For football we had two strips, one red and one green, and we wore dark blue wool shorts that itched. The ball was leather and usually so heavy with dew that headers posed the risk of brain damage. There were goal posts but no nets.

Wolvesey Sports Field. Alasdair on the left, sporting his First XI cricket cap.

In the cricket season we played in our ordinary school clothes unless we were in the First XI when we wore whites. All bats and pads were provided by the school and came with us in a large brown canvas cricket bag which was like an over-sized Gladstone bag. A few boys had their own bats which they lovingly rubbed with linseed oil and 'knocked in', a process that involved hitting it in the 'meat' repeatedly with a composite cricket ball hung from a string in the Priory Stables.

On the short walk to the playing fields from the school gate we passed a gravel carpark under a line of beech trees which usually had a Heinkel and a Messerschmidt, both bubble cars but with names that sparked intense curiosity and a degree of puzzlement that they should be attached to objects so modest. By comparison, British cars were more substantial.I was proud of British cars. Foreign cars were very odd; some even had their engines in the boot. When I heard parents discussing them, they tended to say that parts would be expensive and hard to obtain. Cars needed to be serviced frequently and the 'little man' in the local garage might not understand them. There was also the question of national pride. Buying a foreign car was mildly seditious; you were letting down the side.

My pride in our country was bolstered in our History lessons in which we were given a simple and reassuring view of the world, fostered by Our Island Story, a book now discredited by those who feel confident enough about the present to feel free to disparage the errors of the past. It galloped at breakneck speed, never stopping for breath at the Tudors or the Stuarts but covering the ground from the Romans to the death of Queen Victoria in one hectic dash.

Although the story was not one of unalloyed success, our confidence was not shaken by early defeats at the hands of the Vikings and Romans whose invasions barely registered as losses. Even the Norman Conquest was seen as no more than the start of a new season. Instead we thrilled at the cleverness of English archers who kept their longbows dry at Agincourt, the nerve and sacrifice of Nelson, the victories of Marlborough with his clever phone number, BROM 4689, that was the mnemonic to remember the names and dates of his victories, and the ingenious mechanism in the big guns of the Dreadnought battleships that enabled them to engage in rapid fire. Gosh, we were good wherever you looked. Other countries might be richer or poorer, but no one knew their position as certainly as we did. We had style. We had a tradition of being the winning team. Right was always on our side. People looked up to us because they knew that our institutions had quality.

The only time history was ambiguous was during the period of the English civil war when it was hard to decide who was right and who was wrong. This did not mean we had any doubt about whom we supported. Indeed, as every British schoolboy has always known, we knew with absolute certainty which side we were on. Those boys who were circumcised were Roundheads, and those of us who were not were Cavaliers.

While one might have expected there to be overwhelming support for the King, there being no Jewish or Muslim boys at the school, surprisingly the numbers for and against were approximately equal. The reason for the anomaly was that being circumcised was an indicator of high rank. In hindsight it is puzzling that parents sought to establish a boy's social position by mutilating his genitals, given that the badge would be visible only to a restricted audience, but fashion is often incomprehensible to following generations.

History stopped at the First World War, though our History master occasionally crossed the line, as when he described Bismarck's break-out into the North Atlantic. I was awestruck by the thought of battleships firing off shells the weight of a small car at such long range that they took nearly a minute to arrive. The image of the mighty Hood sinking in seconds because of flash igniting the magazine was both enthralling and appalling.

In a less dramatic tale, the master described how his escort ship in the North Atlantic rolled so wildly that they had to clean the cutlery by ramming it into a tin of Gumption, an abrasive cleaning material, and then wiping it on a cloth. The story might have lacked strategic appreciation, but it painted a vivid picture of the squalor on board a small warship in a mighty sea.

The influence of the Royal Navy was strong. Portsmouth was nearby with the Royal Dockyards and Vospers, famous for making fast torpedo boats, just over the wall of Earwig's back garden. Every Christmas, the choir went to sing at HMS Dolphin, the submarine training base. We Commoners had singing lessons given by a naval officer. Under the oak beams of the classroom in the Priory Stables, we sang 'Hearts of Oak', 'Rule Britannia' and a number of sea shanties including one with a sad line about a cabin boy who, as his ship sinks, imagines his parents weeping for him in Old Portsmouth Town.

Even the biggest and most enduring school craze had a link to the Navy. No one quite knew when it started or ended, but there was great enthusiasm for collecting huge fleets of Triang model warships, each one only a few inches long and made in diecast metal. Having bought their ships, boys would then decide which of two alliances to join, though curiously no one knew who headed the alliances, no permission was required to join, and no record was kept. Despite that, there was much speculation about which fleet would win if there were to be a confrontation, although no thought was given as to how a confrontation might be brought about or how the outcome would be decided. The craze absorbed a great deal of our pocket money so even in that detail it was eerily close to real life.

We spent much of our free time making Airfix and Revel models of Second World War aeroplanes, tanks and ships, trying always to make them 'realistic' by assembling and painting them carefully. There was no higher praise than 'realistic', except possibly 'jolly realistic'.

Aeroplanes were comparatively easy to assemble, but tanks were next to impossible. If you were lucky you would end up with one that looked as if it had had bomb damage, with its tracks blasted off its wheels. Glue was the enemy. It worked by dissolving the plastic at the points of contact so that when it set, they had welded together. One carelessly applied drop, or any oozing excess, would make your finished model look leprous. No paint, however carefully applied, would cover it.

Another danger of glue was that once on your clothing it was impossible to get off without solvents. One evening after prayers, the headmaster told us that a boy had ruined his school jacket by spilling glue on it and instructed us to wear our handicraft aprons if handling glue. The following day I was trying to get my tube of glue to run. Nothing would persuade it. Then it exploded all over my suit jacket. I panicked and hid the jacket in my locker.

For a day or so I managed to cover the loss but then I reported it missing. No one could understand the mystery. In the meantime, I was sick with anxiety and wrote letters to Nancie (who at the time was in Scotland) saying I needed a jacket urgently. The following Sunday when I was away with a friend on a leave-out, a search was ordered of the whole school. Inevitably my jacket was found.

On my return, the headmaster spoke to me as we passed in a corridor and said he thought it was time I told the truth. I broke down and cried. He was far more understanding than I had a right to expect, but the point had been made to me that covering up is worse than facing up honestly to the consequences of one's action. As it turned out, because of the earlier incident, Sister had discovered a solvent that removed the glue with ease.

Not all our models were made of plastic. Sometimes a misguided relative would give a boy an elaborate balsa wood model aircraft for construction, occasionally with a 'jet' engine that worked with a pellet of fuel, though more often it would have a small petrol engine. They were never a success. The patience required to assemble the slender ribs and apply the paper fabric, stretching it taut by applying dope, was far beyond that of the average boy. The finished product would look asymmetric, ragged and limp. Inevitably it would crash to destruction within feet of being launched, to a sympathetic chorus of 'hard cheese' from those who had come to watch.

Far more successful were the 'Sleek Streak' balsa wood models with their bright red markings and rubber band powered propellers that could be bought for 2/11d and assembled and flown within two minutes of being unpacked. Unhappiness was when a maiden flight ended in a gutter. There was no greater joy than to see your model disappear over the roofs only to be turned by a breeze and land safely back in the yard.

In the dark evenings of winter we had competitions to discover who had the most powerful torch. We would shine our beams on distant trees to see whose was brightest. There was a type of torch the shape of a hip flask with a bulbous lens on top like a giant bullseye that always did well, though I liked my rubberised torch that I could shine in the bath. Many torches were destroyed when the batteries leaked. Batteries were traitorous and would eat away an appliance if they were not removed as soon as they had discharged.

Knowledge of sex was referred to as 'being educated' and was a great secret. I eventually got someone to tell me by using the interrogator's ploy of pretending that I knew already. What the boy then told me was not enlightening. A man had to put his P into a woman. I was confused. I had frequently seen Nancie naked and was unaware of any obvious apertures.

At about the same time as I was uncovering life's mysteries, I sat my Eleven Plus exam. Norman had explained to me that it was a useful insurance policy to know that I would be able to go to a grammar school if the money for private education dried up.

Grammar schools are now regarded as hotbeds of privilege encircled by middle-class parents in large four-wheel-drive vehicles intent on preventing hordes of poorer children, thirsty for knowledge, from entering. But that is not how we viewed them. Going to a day school of any sort was to fall out of the Garden of Eden. Going to a grammar school would have been unimaginable ignominy.

An uncle had warned me that the Eleven Plus exam could be tricky, citing the question, 'Which is the odd one out – dog, cat or gun?' According to him, it was the cat because dogs and guns both required licences at that time. I discovered much later in life that my uncle was a member of MENSA, which explains why his answer, though imaginative in a tortured way, was profoundly unhelpful.

In order to take the test, we had to go to a state school, which had the thrill of entering enemy territory. We were given a short briefing that did little more than underline the standing order that if anyone taunted us, we had to ignore them. Thus prepared, we set off with mild apprehension.

The day itself was an anti-climax. We were treated kindly by everyone we met and made to feel welcome. In due course I learned that I had passed the test, though the value of my insurance policy diminished as government policy changed and grammar schools became comprehensive schools.

I cannot say why I was so afraid of the working class, as we hardly ever came across any members of it as we walked through the cathedral close, doffing our caps to members of clergy, parents or staff. There were working-class people employed at the school, polishing our shoes, preparing our food, feeding the boiler and looking after the sports field, but only the maids who poured our tea had speaking parts. They would hold large teapots and hover round our tables at breakfast and high tea asking in an accent we mocked,

'Anyone want any more tigh?' It is not always pleasant to look back at the past.

My fear might well have stemmed from a constant repetition of warnings by people in charge of our well-being that the main purpose in life of 'rough boys' was to beat us up. Indeed, it can only have been these warnings that made me nervous, because I remember not a single time when I was threatened in such a way. The only incident of any sort that I can recall was a minor one. I had a friend whose family lived behind Harrods and owned a Bentley S1, a car with lines of such perfection they have never been surpassed. As the chauffeur was driving us up Regent Street, we were caught in a traffic jam. A boy who was crossing the road put his face up to the car window next to where I was sitting, much as the refugee children used to do in Karachi, and shouted, 'Snobs!' It was scarcely the stuff of trauma and it would be hard to overcome a defence of fair comment.

The trip up to London in the Bentley with my friend Mark was recorded in an excited letter I wrote to my parents after my first experience of affluence. I must have been bubbling to tell them because I wrote it on a Monday.

In my letter I gilded a few facts and omitted others. Mr Coleman was the chauffeur who was sent to Winchester to collect us. The family called him Coleman, but I am pleased I gave him a title. Despite what I wrote, we never reached 100mph, the magic ton, although the speedometer had wavered at around 90mph on the M4, a fact which we faithfully reported to Mark's father, sadly resulting in Coleman being restricted to 60mph for our return to school. There was not yet a speed limit on motorways, so he had not been breaking the law. My parents were presumably meant to know that we had gone to Earls Court to see the 1965 Motor Show.

As we were leaving the show, I was struck by the joy of getting into a warm car on a cold night, nor will I ever forget the sensuousness of that car with its scent of wood, carpet and Connolly hide, and its gentle caress as I leant my head against a soft leather padding that curved from the back seat onto the rear roof pillar under a mirror containing a cigar lighter in its frame.

The house we were staying in was in Walton Street, in Knightsbridge. The 'Bent' lived a stone's throw away in Pont Street Mews.

On the Saturday morning we were each given a generous present of a pound and let loose in Harrods to spend it. Afterwards we went to a matinee performance of Those Magnificent Men in their Flying Machines, a film that, like many of the time, pandered to our belief that we the British were really the soundest of chaps.

In my letter I described the firework display in the back garden that evening as 'lovely', but in truth it was alarming. I am surprised I did not record the drama but there were obviously more important (and less worrying) things I wanted to communicate and 'lovely' dismissed the event efficiently. The problem was that there was a strong wind blowing and as two of the rockets reached roof height, they turned upside down and, while still under full power, crashed into neighbouring gardens, adding to our embarrassment by giving their full flamboyant display at ground level. Surprisingly no one complained, but as it was only just over two decades since the Blitz, people were evidently still blasé about unexpected explosions in their gardens.

Monday.

The Pilgrims School
Winchester.
Hants.

Dear Mother and Father.
On friday Mr Coleman took us up to London. On the M4 we did 100 m.p.h. We went straight to Earls court where we saw all the cars. At the End there was a muddle about our "rendez-vous" which resulted in Mr Walford Walford waiting by the main entrance for 15 mins and Mark running once round the whole building.
When we got home we had steak and then did some shooting.
In the morning we got up at 9 o'clock and had breakfast.

Then we went to buy riches for "those magnificent men in their flying machines".
After a good lunch we saw the film which was marvelous. When we were back home we had a lovely firework display and then went to "vivians" one of the finest restaurants in London. I had a shrimp cocktail and 1 snail that Mark gave me. Then I had a steak that was medium done and a water (ice) When we got home I did some night shooting. On sunday morning we had Breakfast at 9-15 a.m. and

3

Amused ourselves until 10 when we took Sugar the golden spaniel for a walk.
We took him out for 1½ ho and make a rather round about way for Hyde park where he chased the birds. When we got home we had lunch and played about on the trampoline until 6 o'clock when Mr Coleman (driver) took us to the wimpy bar where we had a Wimpy meal. At 6'30 Mr Coleman took us to school but before we went in we had a coke at the Royal Royal.
Love
Thanks for the Anttear. Niall.

A letter written excitedly on a Monday to tell of the trip to London in the Bentley.

'Vivian's' restaurant, where we went for supper on the first night, was in Basil Street, also behind Harrods, and was a place where Mark's father went regularly. Dressed in a suit and wearing Hush Puppy shoes, he puffed on a cigar as we went in, early in the evening before the main service had started. He did not eat with us but sat talking to the proprietor who was a friend. My shrimp cocktail and medium rare steak were right on the zeitgeist. Mark's snails were adventurous. The Wimpy meal the following night was the equal of 'Vivian's' and we had Knickerbocker Glories, tall glasses filled with tinned fruit salad and ice cream which we scooped out with long spoons.

On the trip back to school, as bands of heavy rain swept in and drummed on the car, I sat cocooned in warmth, listening to 'Sing Something Simple' on the car radio. I knew it was luxury and I revelled in it.

Mark was rare in having parents who were happy to be seen to be rich. Boasting, or swanking as we called it, was a cardinal sin, and parents were usually discrete even if there was a title or an ancestral pile lurking in the background.

Politically, most parents supported the Conservative Party, as did mine though they were towards the liberal end, having the normal middle-class conceit that the country was a team run in a common interest. When they saw that the trades unions were letting down the team, they sighed.

Although a Conservative voter, Norman's distrust of the Labour Party leader, Harold Wilson, was based on his judgement of him as a person rather than because he led a left-wing government. He thought him politically crooked, a description Wilson would have taken as a compliment. It gave him great pleasure when television mimics repeatedly used Wilson's catch phrase, 'To be perfectly frank and honest and reasonable' to introduce some particularly fanciful statement that illustrated none of the qualities described. Political satire on television was a satisfying new way of sticking pins into one's adversary.

At school we learned through osmosis that we were born to be Conservatives. So subtle was the influence that I was not even aware of being indoctrinated. When we discussed the different interest groups the political parties represented, we knew instinctively which side we were on. Our loyalty was strong. When, in the 1964 general election, a boy whose parents were both doctors told us they had voted Labour, we were shocked. More accurately, we were stunned. Had he told us they had both been leading Nazis, we could not have been more horrified.

Although my view of the world was still limited, two positions had been shaped by my parents and were strong. The first was that the United States was a force for good. Whenever there were natural disasters, Americans were the first to arrive and had the ability like no others to bring order to chaos. They were fine people with big hearts, and they were a reliable ally. The second was that the State of Israel was to be admired. My parents had visited the country on their way out to Pakistan and had been enormously impressed by the vigour and hard work that young Israelis had put into turning desert into arable land. They often told the story about how a Palestinian taxi driver had stopped near the border to point out that the Israelis had taken all the good land. The difference in quality was indeed stark but to my parents the difference was a testament to effort.

In the absence of any formal teaching about the recent war, most of our knowledge of it came from comics or 'trash' as we called them. They all celebrated British servicemen in the most partisan way. Every week fine British heroes found themselves in jeopardy, though they always prevailed. The opposition might be tough, but the British were tougher still.

Germans, referred to as 'Huns', 'Krauts' or 'Jerry', had a habit of crying out 'Gott im Himmel!' and 'Donner und Blitzen!' before being shot, often with a surprised look on their faces. The Japanese, referred to as 'Japs' or 'Nips', uttered 'Ayyeeee!' or 'Banzai!'. The text boxes for the British pilots were not much better. None of them said the only word which anyone would ever say in combat.

I obtained a more sensible view of a particular aspect of war through the books of Colonel Oreste Pinto who wrote the 'Spycatcher' series about his life as a counter-intelligence officer working for MI5 during the war. His enduring message was that torture is morally despicable and produces unreliable intelligence. Although he was a Dutchman, his nationality was a nicety that I missed. I had no doubt he was speaking for Britain when he said that torture was something we never did and never should do. Ever.

Apart from their war exploits, I was not much interested in our European neighbours, though we boys admired the Germans greatly for their Faller models and electric train sets which were jolly realistic. If there is one thing that surprises me, it is that I cannot recall any anti-German feeling either at school or at home. Norman's family, who had contacts with a German family before the war, picked up where they had left off with exchanges of children and letters. Norman too was pro-German, having become fluent in the language when on a prolonged bicycling holiday along the Rhine shortly before the outbreak of war. He told me that there was nothing intrinsically bad about the German people and that in all societies, including our own, people existed who would be willing to torture and run death camps. The lesson to learn from the war was of the need to protect democracy from the first attack. Once you fear for your life, it is too late.

Anti-Japanese feeling was quite another matter, particularly amongst those who had fought them. I once had lunch with a friend whose father asked me where I had been born. When I told him, he said that he had had a rat's eye view of Burma but spoke the words with such bitterness that I felt I had touched a mains cable. Norman, although never a prisoner of the Japanese, never forgot the severed head of his friend on the parapet of a bridge. He only realised the depth of his loathing of them when he attended a lunch in 1963 in the Divinity Faculty in Edinburgh. The convention was to not leave a space next to anyone already sitting down. When one day he realised he would have to sit next to a Japanese person, he hesitated. It was only for an instant and he overcame his revulsion, but it required a conscious effort to take that necessary step of reconciliation.

My view of Britain as a country of special magnificence that had won the war was reinforced by the set-piece services in the cathedral that took place on Assize Sunday and Remembrance Day, when important people would parade in robes and uniforms. There was a belief in the school that playing the lowest note of the organ would bring about the collapse of the cathedral, but during these services the building showed itself to be impervious to attack. As the first chords of 'All People that on Earth Do Dwell' were sounded, I knew I was in for a ride. By the time we reached the end of the hymn, with the choir singing their hearts out in descant, I could feel the music through my bones. When it stopped, the silence was shocking, and I was left exhilarated and spent.

Religion to me was more a cultural tradition than a vehicle of faith, because I neither challenged nor accepted any of the fundamental beliefs. What I understood were the instructions on the types of desirable behaviour.

On Sunday evenings, instead of prep we did Catechism, writing answers to questions about Christianity, a process designed to give substance to the nebulous by repetition. As no one ever read the answers, I stopped writing them. It was a rare example of subversion without consequence which gave a clue as to the value the school placed on the process.

Despite my lack of application to the Scriptures, I was confirmed by the Bishop of Winchester in the cathedral at the age of twelve, along with girls from St Swithin's who sat across from us on the aisle, virginal in white as well as in body.

Girls were as remote as people in a railway carriage going in the same direction on a parallel line. I had no doubt whatever that one day I would marry a girl and by implication 'do it' with her and have children, certainly in that order, but what the intervening steps would be were far from clear. It did not bother me unduly, as I was quite content without them.

As confirmation presents, I was given a prayer book and a pocket copy of the New Testament both of which were bound in red leather and edged in gold. After being confirmed, we were allowed to get up early on a Sunday to go to communion. Strangely I enjoyed it. Much of the pleasure came from the privilege, but there was something special about being in a small group of people in the early morning light, listening to the murmur of the cleric's voice as he hastened through the service, cutting in sharply after the mumbled responses in an attempt to press the pace, each word smothering the echo of the one before.

At the time that I was embarking on my journey to spiritual fulfilment and in contradiction to its objectives, I bullied a boy. The school had been increasing in size and there were no longer enough beds in the dormitories for the number of boarders, so friends of the school who lived nearby rented out rooms to take the overflow. The boy I bullied shared a bedroom with me in an old terraced house on a street just outside the cathedral close.

There was no justification for me to behave as badly as I did. The reason was trivial. I had hoped that I would be sharing with one of my friends, so was disappointed when I found I was not. What started as a sulky niggling became aggressive and unkind. I even encouraged my friends to be poisonous to him.

The boy must have complained to his parents because the headmaster approached me and said he had heard that I was being a bully and that my behaviour had to change immediately. The seriousness of the matter was conveyed by the tone of his voice and the look of steel in his eyes. There was no formality to the discussion. No prearranged meeting. No rehearsal of facts. No record of the conversation. No written commitment from me to mend my ways. It was all over in two minutes, but it was the slap across the face that I needed. Not only did I stop but I made certain that my friends stopped too. It was as simple as throwing a switch.

One legitimate way of giving someone a physical beating was in the boxing ring. When I first went to the school, my parents insisted that I take up the sport because it would help me look after myself, presumably if any of those rough boys who stood on street corners ever stopped talking to each other for long enough to pick a fight with me. My parents might also have thought that I needed a bit of toughening up. I was painfully shy, to the extent of being too anxious even to go into a shop on my own. Nancie had had a frank talk with me and told me that shyness was an unattractive quality and that I needed to overcome it. She and Norman must have thought that if I could knock seven bells out of someone in the ring, then my shyness would evaporate.

Boxing instruction was given in the gymnasium at Winchester College by a retired sergeant major. Although I can still remember many of the techniques he taught me, they were of limited use because my regular opponent, who was also my best friend, fought in an unorthodox style, making conventional tactics hard to put into effect. Instead of jabbing punches at me in the way that we had been instructed, he approached with his arms flailing, like someone trying to practise the front crawl. This made it easy for me to defend by the simple expedient of putting up a forearm. Having brought his flailing to a stop, I could then jab blows to his chest at will, theoretically building up points until we ended up in a bearhug.

Ours was always the last bout in any contest but it was the most popular. The other boys looked forward to seeing what they called the 'paddle steamer' fight because it was so chaotic. Sergeant Major must have regarded our approach as a sacrilege not worth judging because he always pronounced the result to be a tie.

Sergeant Major also taught shooting, which took place in the A-framed space of an attic room. We would lie at the entrance on padded canvas mats and fire air rifles at targets illuminated dramatically at the far end by two light bulbs protected by aluminium guards in the shape of scallop shells. Either side of the range were stored our trunks.

I was a reasonably good shot, but during one inter-school competition I was wildly off form.

The procedure for the competition was to practise on ordinary targets and, when you felt you were ready, slot in the competition ones that bore the official stamps. After you had fired, Sergeant Major had to sign the target and send it off to the organising authority.

My practice results were dreadful and deteriorated further after the competition target had been put in. Distraught, I rose slowly to my feet only to hear Sergeant Major congratulating me on getting a perfect score. It was then that I saw he was casually using his thumb and forefinger to press an air pellet repeatedly through the bull's eye at the centre of my competition target. I was later awarded a medal for shooting. It was made of some base medal and stayed in my cufflink box until I lost it.

In addition to using the Winchester College gymnasium, we also swam in their pool, Gunners' Hole, which was no more than a dammed section of the River Itchen. The water flowed from the river through a sluice and was unheated. Each day the temperature was chalked up in Fahrenheit on the wooden fence by the entrance which you approached with a gambler's hope. Often the figure would be in the mid-fifties, which is a point at which hypothermia becomes an urgent concern when saving life at sea, but after a prolonged period of hot weather, the temperature might rise to the high sixties or on rare occasions break the magic seventy.

For a swimming pool, it was unusual in being curved as it followed a bend in the river. Its sides were lined with stone or concrete, giving it shape and structure, but the base was left as the original riverbed, not that anyone looking down from above could see it through the dark water. Sometimes on a sunny day, if I did a surface dive wearing googles, I could see the weeds swaying over the white chalk floor and even minnows and eels. On either side of the pool was a wide area of grass, shielded from public view by a tall wooden fence built in a rough ellipse round the perimeter. Up against the fence were thatched changing areas, individual changing cubicles not being necessary because the Winchester College boys bathed with no clothes. A photograph on the internet shows that in the 1930s, even their masters bathed naked, unless one of the sixth form boys was bald and had middle-age spread.

The water in Gunners' Hole was dark and cold, making swimming a raw and wholesome experience. Pre-Raphaelites would have planted water lilies on the black surface and floated young women with flowing red hair and alabaster skin. DH Lawrence would have stripped and plunged into the deep, especially if the Pre-Raphaelite women were already there. But for all its natural attractions, the water left us shivering. Fortunately, the school rule was compassionate and required only that boys enter the pool at least once each session, even if just for a baptismal dip.

Stars were awarded for achievement in swimming and diving and were sewn onto our Speedos. Everyone wore Speedos; there were no other costumes. Colours in the form of a stitched shield in the shape of a scallop shell, the size of a blazer badge, were given for lifesaving, taking up any remaining space. The convention was to put stars to the left, leaving room on the right for the colours badge to avoid it looking like a codpiece. The overall effect was as subtle as a dictator's uniform, but the visibility of achievement encouraged competition, even if it also attracted a certain amount of attention when swimming in public pools.

Gunners' Hole

The diving boards were named with simplicity and candour. The springboards were 'Little Willy' and 'Big Willy' and the four cubes that stood like a winner's podium were 'Matchboxes'. Hidden amongst trees to prevent the Winchester College boys from outraging public decency, were the highest diving boards. The lowest and longest was 'Railway Track', above it was 'Sen' and up in the clouds was 'Sen Sen

In my last year I won a diving cup. The final dive was off Railway Track which, although only eight feet high, was considerably higher than anything I had dived off before. The competition took place in the afternoon and even at lunchtime I had reservations about taking part because I was frightened. Fortunately, I was persuaded and obtained nearly full marks for the dive. My parents witnessed it and said that it should persuade me that I could cope with any challenge life threw in my direction. In a strange way they were right.

Swimming Colours

Somewhat to my surprise, I had been made Head Commoner, which was a great honour and meant my name went up on a board, where no doubt it still is, four years behind Alasdair's. I had a modest amount of power and could make people report themselves to a master or to Sister if they were breaking the school rules or offering me cheek. Mostly, the role meant I had duties, particularly making sure that at night the external gates were locked and that the lights were switched off in all the buildings.

The main benefit from being senior in the school was that for our meals we sat at the headmaster's table with other staff members and their spouses. We were treated without condescension, and the conversation was often lively and amusing, giving me a soft social skill that was to prove as valuable as anything else I learned at school. It was the final polish.

The Charles Cup for Diving

CHAPTER 5

Back from Pakistan

In 1961, at the end of my second term at school, Alasdair and I flew out to Pakistan for Christmas, this time to Rawalpindi. My parents had moved there in the autumn because Norman's job was to sell to the Pakistani government a pipeline from the newly discovered natural gas plant in Sui, in the middle of the desert.

It was my last flight in a BOAC Comet. After a long delay in Rome, we landed at Cairo. The pyramids, sharp in the early morning sun and still in open desert, slipped down the starboard side of the aircraft as we wallowed in on final approach, bouncing on the first thermals of the day. After we landed, Alasdair and I sat in a cafeteria patiently drinking Coca Cola while the technical hitch was fixed.

At Karachi we were met by a company employee who arranged our transfer to a PIA Fokker Friendship and gave me the unwelcome present of a basket containing my cat, Lilibet.

The light was fading as we made the final leg of our journey. I hated every moment of that flight. My cat never stopped meowing, even for an instant, and I was consumed with anxiety that the wing was burning off when as the sky darkened into night, I could see a blue flame emerging from the engine.

It was to be our last trip to Pakistan. Norman was nearly fifty years old, an age at which expatriate jobs came to an end and people were expected to return to the UK head office of Burmah in London, assuming there was a position available.

The idea of working in London held no appeal, especially as Alasdair and I had been entered to go to Fettes College in Edinburgh for our secondary education. Norman had felt deeply frustrated being far away from the family in the year leading up to Deborah's death and he never wanted the family to be far apart again. Edinburgh was the city that had been our home and was the natural choice.

His decision to train as a minister in the Church of Scotland stemmed not from a strong religious calling but more from a desire to do social good and be his own master within an established structure. There was much in the creed that he regarded as gobbledegook, inserted over the years by people embellishing a simple truth. As far as the Virgin Birth was concerned, he liked to point out that the Greek Gods were forever inseminating virgins. As for the afterlife, he had no better insight than anyone who has ever lived but was sceptical.

He did not discuss his decision with Nancie until, shortly before leaving Karachi, she found a letter from the theological college in Edinburgh, inviting him to interview when he next had home leave. It was the first she knew about it and she was upset by the uncharacteristic betrayal. He explained that he had not wanted to open the subject until he knew he had a reasonable chance of being accepted.

As soon as the proposition was out in the open and they could discuss it, they realised they would require two incomes. Apart from any other considerations, Nancie was eleven years younger than Norman and with great prescience they thought she needed to have an income of her own in case she was widowed early.

Teaching was an obvious profession for Nancie as it would leave her free during the holidays and domestic science an obvious subject as it would give her the household skills she had not acquired, having grown up in institutions and having had servants during most of her adult life.

Alasdair and I knew nothing of these plans, nor did we know that this was to be our final trip. For us, it was just the school holiday.

It was a whistle-stop month. Our driver Saeed, a wiry paratrooper in the Pakistani army, took us in our Chevrolet Impala up to the hill station of Murree, a journey of some three hours in each direction. A calm man, he had such control of the car that it never seemed to accelerate, turn or brake, but simply glided. Often, the only way I knew how fast we had been going was when the car slowed to a town speed limit and gave the illusion it had eased to walking pace.

It was cold when we arrived in the late afternoon, and there was snow on the peaks. The light was fading as we made our way through the crowds in the bazaar, past stalls lit by oil lamps selling cheap goods I didn't want to buy, even though I had money in my pocket.

A few days later, early in the morning, we flew to Peshawar in the Burmah Oil Company aircraft, a de Havilland Dove, with the family of the friends who had first introduced Nancie to a sweaty rugby man in Rangoon. When we landed, Saeed and their driver were waiting for us on the tarmac with our cars.

We picked up a military convoy and drove through the Khyber Pass, stopping at the Khyber Rifles barracks where we were met by a military pipe band, entertained to lunch and made honorary members of the Khyber Rifles mess. Every time we stopped the cars to look at the barren scenery, our escorts got out of their Land Rovers and covered the surrounding terrain with their weapons. We had been told that if we stepped off the tarmacked road, within the rules of the game, we could be shot by tribesmen.

In the afternoon, we returned to Peshawar where, in the hustle of the bazaar, my parents bought the lamps, bowls and plates that were to become tangible evidence of their past.

Later, we had tea with the German consul who proudly showed us his stereogram and played a record on it, encouraging us to make out the different instruments coming out of each speaker. He insisted on driving us back to the airport in his Mercedes-Benz which had a novel speedometer that showed the speed as changing blocks of colour against a scale. The more he showed off his toys, the more I sensed that the adults in our group were becoming irritated.

Our final trip was to the gas plant in Sui. Apart from the plant itself, there was little there. The runway was unsurfaced and there was limited accommodation. The purpose of the trip was notionally related to business, but Norman and his boss had added on an excursion with a woman called Sylvia Schofield to visit the Bugti tribe. In her obituary in the *Daily Telegraph*, she was described as 'an agony aunt, wartime intelligence operative, honorary colonel in the US Military Police, advertising copywriter, mystery novelist, photographer, archaeologist and intrepid traveller'. We knew her in her last two capacities.

The reason this redoubtable woman was in the middle of a desert in Pakistan was that she had married a petroleum engineer whom she had met when she had gone out to report on the discovery of natural gas. Living there would have been a challenge for many people, but she made use of the unusual situation to write and to study the Bugtis, a tribe that lived outside the jurisdiction of the Pakistani government. They could do anything they liked, including kill people, as long as they stayed within their area. Sylvia had arranged for us to have lunch with them.

We piled into some stripped-down Land Rovers, with open sides and canvas roofs, and set off excitedly in anticipation of an adventure. We must have followed a compass bearing or possibly some old tracks because there were no roads. From time to time we had to stop and engage four-wheel drive to make our way over some obstacle but eventually we arrived at a fort. As we went through the arched entrance, there was a ragged volley of welcome as the Bugti men fired off their weapons.

The Bugtis could not have been more hospitable. Their leader was sadly not present as he had been unwise enough to commit a murder outside his area and had been detained by the authorities. Lamb had been cooked over hot stones. Afterwards, they gave us rides on their camels.

As we travelled back to Sui, I was taken aback when Norman said that any one of the hospitable warriors would happily have slit our throats under different circumstances. I had thought that because we were British, we were able to see events through a protective glass.

In between our trips, life at home was quiet. Unlike Karachi, there was no beach to go to at the weekend and Alasdair and I spent most of our time in the compound. Nancie had a number of Pakistani women friends who, on their visits to the house, embarrassed me by looking at my golden hair and cooing, 'Isn't he sweet?' as if somehow I wasn't there. I learned with horror of the practice of purdah after Nancie came back in distress, having visited a friend who was forbidden by her father to be seen by men outside the family.

Alasdair and I left Pakistan on a Qantas Boeing 707, the fate of the Comet now sealed by its American cousin. The serried rows of seats were evidence that revenue had ousted glamour, leaving a memory of a golden age of air travel, the gilt applied with a taxpayer's brush.

As I seemed capable of being anxious about any aspect of flying, it is not surprising that I was disturbed to see that on the Boeing the engines were attached to the wings by slender pylons that seemed wholly inadequate. Had anyone told me that they were designed to break off and fall free in the event of extraordinary vibration, I would probably not have boarded.

Alasdair and I never flew back to Pakistan again, although my parents remained until the summer. For our next school holidays at Easter we stayed with our grandparents who lived in Lymington, a Georgian town on the south coast of England at the mouth of the Lymington river, looking across to the Isle of Wight.

Val had been forced to retire from Burma Railways in January 1948 just after the country became independent. The dismissal was put into effect with brutal suddenness. British workers were no longer wanted. It was a bitter moment for them, especially for Kathleen who had lived in the country almost continuously for forty-three years and for whom it was her home.

Many in the United Kingdom now heap opprobrium on empire and, like collaborators denouncing their neighbours, condemn those who worked for it as having the morals of pirates. But my grandparents' love of the culture and people they lived with was genuine and strong.

In retirement they pined for Burma. Naming their house 'Chinthays' after the Burmese lions was but a small visible sign. Burma shaped conversation and provided inspiration for Kathleen's creative needlework and writings. Anywhere you looked in the house, you could see the lacquer work and beaten Burmese silverware which was the shrine to their past. In their conversations with each other, they used Burmese words, as if sharing memories of a lost child. It was the deepest love. As Kathleen wrote some years later, 'Maybe, according to our way of thinking, the Burmese were muddlers, but they wanted to do things in their own way, without other people's interference. As something of a muddler myself, I'd hate someone else to organise me.' As a pirate, Kathleen was unconvincing.

Lymington had spread along the river, its houses evolving round boatyards in an anarchy of faded brickwork, greying oak and painted plaster, threaded with ivy, thorn and privet. Each building was of individual character, some ugly and others handsome, forming a collective beauty, each a dot on a canvas that had grown slowly to create a harmony of imperfection.

Moving inland, you could see where an urgent need for houses had required an alien crop to be planted in farmland fields. Styled by people to whom Lymington was only a name, made with materials from elsewhere and differing from each other only in the number on the door, they had arrived to satisfy a need for shelter. In time, individuality would triumph in small ways – a covered porch, an added room, a change of tiling, climbing flowers on the wall – as the newcomers adjusted to local ways, but it would take many generations before irregularity would root it into the landscape. Until that time, they would remain the new estate. A place to live but not a place that yet belonged.

The house my grandparents bought had been recently built on a private road in Woodside, overlooking open fields. It was of cheap red-brick construction with dark blue woodwork that gave it the simple honesty of a child's construction kit. The thin walls, metal-framed single-glazed windows and lack of insulation meant that it was hot in summer and cold in winter, but it had a pleasing balance and sat comfortably on a large plot, surrounded by privet hedge. While it lacked the timbered beams and kitchen range that soothe the English middle class, its modest functionality represented luxury and security for two people who as refugees had owned only the contents of a single suitcase.

The house was furnished with wartime utility furniture of plain design. On the ground floor, the sitting room could just accommodate a sofa, two chairs, a desk and a wooden window seat. It felt snug if another couple was invited for a glass of sherry. Any more than that created a stilted politeness as people pretended others had a greater right to sit than they and everyone remained standing, pressed awkwardly together.

The dining room had a table that could just seat six and was used every day because the kitchen was too small to eat in. It was a tight fit. If anyone wanted to enter or leave the room during a meal, people had to shuffle their chairs in to let the person pass. At breakfast, a wireless on the sideboard played the news on the Home Service and it was wise not to talk. From time to time Val would mutter something in ancient Greek.

The kitchen had a solid fuel boiler that was fed with coke and produced only hot water; there was no central heating. Next to the boiler was a grey, wrought-iron gas cooker with an eye level grill on which I made the toast, which was highly praised for its consistent quality. Being too young to realise that I was being manipulated, I was rather pleased. Beside the cooker was a stack for pans and a unit that Val had made out of aluminium. On the other side of the room were a deep, white ceramic sink and a larder. There was no fridge.

Adjoining the kitchen was a toilet that could be converted to a darkroom to develop photographs, and which contained all the necessary chemicals and equipment, neatly stored on shelves.

Upstairs there were three small bedrooms – each little bigger than the double beds they contained – and a tiled bathroom, the small white tiles the size of chocolate bars. On the landing was a ladder that could be brought down using a pole with a hook on the end of it that enabled Alasdair and me to climb up into the attic where we slept on camp beds. We could easily have been accommodated in the other rooms, but my grandparents believed that we needed a space to which we could retreat. There was a window from which we could look out to the Solent and a wind-up gramophone on which we played 'Sir Roger de Coverley', 'Ruler of the Queen's Navee', 'Goosey Goosey Gander' and other 78 rpm shellac classics. There were many books, including the whole series about Orlando the Marmalade Cat. As cats went, he never seemed to be short of money and gave the impression he came from a smart cat family which did things in style.

One of the benefits of being in the attic was that in the morning I could look down on the landing and watch the comings and goings below as people made their way to and from the bathroom, shouting out 'Bathroom free!' when they had finished. Val wore a leather strop round his waist which he used for honing the blade of his cut-throat razor.

My grandparents had paid cash for the house, which used up much of their capital. They, along with many others, had patriotically bought war bonds only to be rewarded by a precipitous decline in their value, reducing their retirement nest egg from ostrich to quail. Despite that, they were contented.

One of the sacrifices they made was to give up their car. In Burma, Val had always enjoyed having a large car which he himself maintained, but when he and Kathleen moved to Lymington, they bought bicycles.

At the start of our holiday, Alasdair and I would go to the bike shed to find our bicycles, his black and mine maroon. Neither bike was new. The word 'bicycle' was never uttered in our family without the qualifying adjectives 'good' and 'second-hand' preceding it. Both bikes had wooden boxes on the back carrier, naturally made by Val, who made everything. Even bolts and nuts were turned on his lathe.

In Edinburgh or Winchester, I was never allowed to wander beyond particular streets on my own. In Lymington I had no constraints other than my willingness to pedal and the requirement to return in time for meals. If I wanted to explore a lane or a track along the sea wall, I could.

A child, free to roam and observe, absorbs beauty as naturally as learning speech. Without guidance as to what my feelings should be or knowledge of Latin and or even vulgar names, I inhaled the lushness of southern England. As I passed houses rooted in the ground, their outside walls changing with the seasons and their driveways green stubbled between car tracks, I knew that this was where I belonged.

Meals at my grandparents' house were simple and wholesome, prepared with vegetables grown in the garden whenever the season allowed. Nothing was bought if it could be made or grown at home, though occasionally there was interest in some modern way of doing things, as when they discovered the surprising novelty of buying a whole chicken in a tin, complete with its jellified juices.

We seldom ate anything sweet, though one September I found that by filling up large jam tins with blackberries from the bushes that grew near the coastal path by the old salterns, I could coerce Kathleen into making blackberry and apple pudding. Helpfulness too can be manipulative.

At Easter, I saw children of my age sailing small, light boats called Moths in the enclosed waters of the Salterns. Unlike the Solent, where Val sailed in his heavy clinker-built boat, it was a safe place for novices to learn to sail. Those who capsized were able to stand, the water being little deeper than the depth required to let the boats float with their centreboards down.

The little sailing club was organised for people who lived locally and owned their own boats. There were no boats available for hire to outsiders, no instructors waiting to give guidance for an hourly fee. If you were not born into a family which had a Moth or were not a friend of someone who owned one, you were destined to stay on the land.

One afternoon, I could bear the exclusion no longer and rushed home to Kathleen, inventing a story that I had been invited onto a boat and it had capsized. She looked at me, standing bone dry in the dining room where she was making a dress on the table, and said with her most condescending tone, 'Yes, dear.' I persisted, setting off another string of 'Yes, dear'. Humiliated, I went back to the Salterns, cross enough to overcome my shyness, and asked a boy who was already wet from a capsize if I could go out in a boat with him. I returned to Chinthays and stood on the doorstep dripping wet with salt water, expecting Kathleen to be impressed. I told her a suitably elaborated story, but as I spoke she chuckled away, constantly repeating 'Yes, dear, yes, dear'. Then she told me to have a bath. She was very loving, but she could be intensely irritating.

Val's dinghy was only 12 feet long, though it seemed to me enormous. It was heavy for its size with its solid wooden construction, metal centre plate and canvas sails. In early spring he would sand it down and apply varnish to the dark hull and light blue paint to the decking. The family would then gather round to push it the mile or so to the Royal Lymington Yacht Club where he had a mooring.

Norman's nickname for Val was Popeye. It was as apt as it was obvious. Both loved sailing, had prominent chins, were wiry, wore sailing hats and smoked pipes. Unlike the real Popeye, Val wore shorts all year round, except when he went to Scotland where even in summer he wore long trousers, because he knew it would be cold.

From time to time, under pressure from Kathleen, Val took Alasdair and me out sailing. It was never an experience I enjoyed because I was frightened for almost all of the time and thought only of drowning.

After rowing to the boat, we put out our hands to fend off as we moved the tender cautiously round the gunwales, while Popeye unhooked and then removed the canvas that went over the boom and covered the cockpit.

If the wind was in the usual direction from the south-west, we had to sail close-hauled down the river before going out into the Solent. The boat heeled over on its side as its centre plate dug in to stop us skidding off downwind. This was naturally another experience that I found terrifying, as the lee deck came dangerously close to the water and we seemed to be in imminent danger of capsizing. Val's reply to my anxious questioning was that action and reaction were equal and opposite. I didn't find it reassuring, partly because I didn't understand what he was saying and partly because any immutable law surely also applied to the little Moths in the Salterns and they blew over in a sneeze. All I could do was cling to my cork lifejacket and calculate how far I would have to swim to the shore if what seemed so inevitable happened. Once out into the Solent, the situation became even worse as we plunged into waves and were soaked by cold, salty water. Fortunately, this produced such an evident display of misery on my part that Val would often relent and turn for home. The wind would now be behind us, its apparent strength reduced, and the boat would return to the upright with its centre plate almost fully raised. At that point I would stop making my calculations and even manage a weak smile.

Alasdair and I returned to Lymington with our parents at the end of the summer term in 1962 when they came home from Pakistan for the last time. We stayed briefly in Chinthays, enjoying the sun and the warm weather before getting into our grey Ford Consul and driving north to our new home in Edinburgh.

We started the journey early in the morning with my grandparents waving us off while still in their night clothes. Every last inch of the car was filled, and it sat low on its springs. With the choke pulled fully out, the cold engine emitted oil-rich fumes while we said our final goodbyes. As soon as we reached the end of the road and wound the windows up after waving our farewells, Nancie passed round the Smith's Potato Crisps with the blue sachet of salt.

There was no motorway network that we could use, and the journey took two days with an overnight stop in Warrington with an aunt and uncle. It was a tedious grind. The car whined in intermediate gears for much of the time but occasionally we had an exciting burst of speed up to sixty or even seventy miles an hour along short sections of dual carriageway. It was hard to tell exactly how fast we were going because in our Ford, the speedometer was a narrow oblong with a needle that only pretended to be accurate in the middle range of speed.

Lorries were a particular problem. Few of them had turbochargers, the device that with magical effect transforms a diesel engine from an emaciated nag into a Suffolk Punch. As a result, they would falter at any incline and drop down one gear after another until they were crawling.

Being in the car was not relaxing with all four of us craning our necks in unison, like a platoon of tortoises doing an 'eyes right', as we tried to see when it might be safe to try to pass the vehicle in front. A missed opportunity was a disappointment and Norman, being a more cautious driver than Nancie, disappointed more than she. Every time she took over the driving, my spirits rose at the thought of some verve and excitement. Sadly, she had a tendency to give in too easily to Norman's pretended concern when he asked if she was still all right to drive. But even Nancie at her competitive best could not hasten us on our way for long. Every overtake was a false summit and, after a brief glimpse of the open road, we would take our place once again behind the slower cars in front, led by the inevitable gravel lorry.

The air inside the car was often foetid. The only ventilation came from winding down the windows or from quarterlights, so the choice was between sitting in a calm fug or the turbulence of a full gale. Demisting was rudimentary and only a few expensive cars had heated rear windows.

Encountering rain was like flying into cloud until someone found the chamois leather.

Little thought had been given to the design of the seats, possibly because the capacity of a car to take passengers was constrained only by ambition. Many cars, including ours, had a single front 'bench' seat upholstered in smooth plastic, a material that chilled you in winter and burned your thighs in summer. Worse still, it was almost frictionless which meant that passengers had to brace themselves to avoid being flung around like an unrestrained ship's piano in a rolling sea.

After two days' travel, we arrived in Edinburgh where we had rented a small basement flat in Heriot Row from some artist friends who lived above it. We called it the Mole Hole.

Compared with the prettiness of Lymington, the soot-stained buildings of the Georgian New Town appeared austere. The uniformity of the façades, so vital to the harmony of the design, had been breached in some cases by the painting of window frames and astragals dark green instead of white which had become the fashionable choice. In other cases, the breach was caused by replacing the astragalled panes with plain plate glass, an effect which gouged out the eyes of the building, leaving empty sockets. More serious transgressions resulted from the conversion of residential houses into offices, when any indignity could be inflicted in the name of practicality. The dominant colour was grey; on many days a perfect camouflage against the sky.

We parked on the cobbled street and went down to the front door of the basement, treading carefully on the slimy stone stairs. The windows had bars to prevent burglars from entering or, as Norman pointed out, occupants from escaping fire.

Alasdair and I shared a room at the front of the flat, from which we could look up at pedestrians walking by the railings from 'restricted view' seats that allowed us to see only their legs. He had a single bed and I a chair that converted into a bed, a compromise betrayed by a lack of arms and the flatness of its three hinged squares of foam. The drawback of the arrangement was that I had to make my bed every night using sheets and blankets, a chore that I put off by staying up late. Unlike most of the furniture in the house, which had been acquired for very little at auction, my chair had been bought new which meant there was despair from my parents when shortly after we had acquired it, one of its thin, splayed legs snapped off while Alasdair and I were rough-housing. When money is tight, waste hurts. From then on, the corner of the chair with the missing leg was supported by a pile of books.

The second room at the front of the flat was the bathroom. Although south facing, its window was constantly in the shadow of the bridging platform that spanned the gap between the front door of the main house and the street. The gloom was maintained by the dark green linoleum flooring and the limited glow of the single bulb hanging in the centre of the ceiling. Along one wall was an enamelled cast iron bath with brass taps and ornamental legs.

At the back of the flat was my parents' bedroom, a few feet larger in each direction than a double bed. Opposite it was a room large enough to take a small table, a desk and some comfortable chairs. It was there that my parents studied together, Norman for his course at the divinity college and Nancie for hers at the Atholl Crescent School of Domestic Science. Off that room was a galley kitchen where above the sink Nancie had hung her copy of the prayer of Sir Francis Drake. The line 'until it be thoroughly finished, which yieldeth the true glory' was heavily underlined in a vain attempt to shame us into acknowledging that not every pot and pan needed to be left in the sink to soak. We never used the term 'passive aggression', but Nancie had it down to a fine art.

There was no view from the front of the flat, other than onto the coal cellars of the basement and the legs of passers-by. Out of the back, we could see the tenements of Jamaica Street, originally built to house the servants of nearby houses but now degraded into slums. Occasionally Alasdair and I descended into the gloomy sub-basement past the old wine bins and went out into the dank garden, where we collected beer cans and bottles that had been thrown over the wall. I was critical of the uncouth behaviour of the people who lived in the slums and frightened by their behaviour but felt no compassion for their plight. They were as unseen as the families who lived in our servants' quarters in Karachi.

The garden was not a place to sit in and enjoy. The sun never reached it and just to inhale the air was to invite tuberculosis. Besides, the thought that a hundred pairs of eyes might be watching from the backs of the houses that looked onto it was enough to induce paranoia in even the most mentally robust. The garden's ostensible purpose was to dry clothes on the lines that ran between stout metal poles, but if ever it had been put to that use, the clothes would have rotted.

Alasdair and I accepted the change in our fortunes without complaint. Our family had been used to moving from house to house and to lodging with grandparents. Anywhere we were was home.

There were benefits. We could watch television for the first time since Deborah died. We had the same 405 line, black and white set which offered a choice of two channels, BBC and ITV. The best hope of a reasonably sharp picture – our indoor aerial never produced one that was completely clear – was to wander around the room while rotating the aerial. As people joked, the best image was obtained while standing on a chair in the middle of the room with one's hand fully extended, so a compromise had to be accepted. The joke always raised a laugh because it was true.

There was a general concern in society about the impact of television on domestic life. People feared that it would lead to the end of reading, culture and the family itself. They also railed against the aesthetic affront of outside aerials as they began to appear on chimney stacks, their wires dangling untidily down the sides of buildings before entering the houses through holes drilled in window frames.

Some of the fears were justified. The aerials turned urban landscapes into cold war listening posts, though most people accepted the change as the price of a good picture.

There were no domestically available recording devices. Programmes became the drill sergeants that marched the country in unison. If they coincided with a mealtime, they often dictated that the meal had to be eaten on the lap in front of the screen, though not in our family.

There were many benefits from television. In earlier years, radio had allowed millions of people to share experiences for the first time and television now made those experiences more vivid. The people who appeared on 'the box' became part of a national family whose fortunes could be openly discussed. The newsreaders, Richard Baker, Kenneth Kendall, Michael Aspel and Robert Dougall were like favourite uncles, their voices free of regional accent, their demeanours authoritative, polite and restrained. They were infinitely reassuring. Listening to them reading the late news induced sleep as effectively as a warm milky drink.

Neither channel broadcasted anything during the day other than a test card and music, the only exception being on Saturdays when there were sports programmes in the afternoon. On Sundays there was heavy emphasis on the religious with live broadcasts of unusually large church congregations singing self-consciously because they were on the telly.

Alasdair and I were undiscriminating in our viewing. Most nights, we watched everything from the first programmes in the early evening until broadcasting came to an end at about eleven o'clock. The close was signalled by a lugubrious prayer from a clergyman, followed by the playing of the national anthem. As the last note faded, the picture would shrink to a white dot which, like the warning to mind the gap on the Tube, developed a fame it had never sought. When the dot had disappeared, one of us would get out of bed to switch off the set which by that time, from the heat of its valves, would be almost too hot to touch. We would then drift off to sleep to the sound of its contractions.

My first winter in the Mole Hole was the infamous one of 1962/63 during which the temperature never rose above zero for three months. As it was the first for three years that

I had not spent under a blazing sun in Pakistan, the contrast was extreme.

Snow did not fall until after Christmas and when it did, it lay unthawed. Much of the country was paralysed. On the television news it looked thrilling, especially as I had found a socket to an external aerial next to our bedroom window and we now had a reliably sharp picture. In the West Country, communities were cut off for weeks. Steam trains were lost in snow drifts and locomotives sent to pull them out were lost too. Farmers plunged through white landscapes rescuing sheep from the snow and animals were fed by helicopter. In the towns and cities, cars slid like hovercraft and when they finally lost all traction, were pushed by helpful people. All normal rules inhibiting social interaction were abandoned, and no one was expected to do much work unless they were flying helicopters, digging animals out of snowdrifts or reading the news. It was the best of times.

Edinburgh continued to function, if not normally, at least with supplies of food and fuel arriving reliably enough to avoid shortages. When it was delivered, milk might be frozen in the bottle with its foil lid raised high like a jack-in-the-box, but at least it was on the doorstep.

In the Mole Hole, our struggle was to stay warm. Heating our flat was not a matter of pressing a button and waiting for warmth to exude from radiators. The task was a cottage industry of different appliances.

The main form of heating was provided by three paraffin heaters each of which promised to provide generous heat for a penny an hour, a fact advertised on billboards. They were effective at warming the two main rooms and the long dark hall, though they produced so much moisture that the condensation on the single-glazed windows dripped and pooled in lakes on the window ledges.

A full tank would keep a heater going for most of the day. Alasdair and I were supposed to check the fuel levels regularly, but we often neglected to do so. As a result, the stoves sometimes burned dry and consumed their wicks, releasing an acrid smell as they smouldered.

The three stoves had a considerable appetite for paraffin. I would walk with Alasdair up the hill to the ironmongers, Gray's of George Street, carrying our two-gallon cans to have them filled from a pump at the back of the shop. The cost would naturally be put on account. Everything went on account. At the butcher, the baker, the greengrocer or the department store, I gave my name and address and it went on the slate. No identification was needed. Your word was enough.

On our return to the house, we were supposed to switch the paraffin heaters off and let them cool down before refilling them, but I became adept at pouring the fuel into them through a funnel while they were still burning. Had I remembered the iron bars on the window, I might have been less cavalier.

In addition to the paraffin heaters, Alasdair and I had a cream-coloured coal stove in our bedroom though we were well into the winter before it was put to use. With a logic that dismayed us, our parents refused to let us light it, explaining that the chimney might have to be swept which would mean troubling the friends who were so kindly renting the flat to us. Fortunately, the matter was resolved to everyone's satisfaction when in conversation with our landlords they expressed astonishment that we were not already using it. Better to be stupid than presumptive.

Our final line of defence against the cold was provided by a radiant electric heater which we used in the mornings to warm our clothes when the stove was dead, and the paraffin heaters had not yet been filled and lit for the day. Although it was convenient to us, requiring neither a short trip to the coal cellar nor a longer one to Gray's of George Street, we were rationed in our use of it, as it was a well-known fact that the cost of running electric heaters was ruinous.

Once the snow had fallen, Alasdair and I took our sledge out into the communal gardens across the street at the front of the house and tobogganed down an icy slope until it got dark. We might have spoken to other children in the gardens, but we didn't learn their names or strike up a friendship with them. Our roots never stretched beyond our school.

I played in the snow in the same clothes I normally wore around the house. With the exception of my knee-length brown corduroy shorts, they were all made of wool. Even my prickly underwear was woollen. In mid-afternoon, I would return to the Mole Hole with Alasdair, my clothes heavy with water. We would share a bath, each lying in our ordained place, according to the rules of precedence.

Now that they were studying at home all day, my parents re-entered my life like rested characters revived in a soap. Apart from the four months I had spent in Karachi, I had seen them for only ten weeks a year since the age of five. Now I could see them for sixteen.

My memories of the time in the Mole Hole are shuffled, only those of the snow and cold being fixed by the notoriety of that winter.

I was still at school in Hampshire but returned to Edinburgh for four weeks both at Christmas and Easter and eight over the summer. For a year, I travelled with Alasdair until he moved school but after that I made the journey on my own, usually by Pullman so that I would be served meals at my place without having to find a dining car.

At the end of the summer term, my parents would drive down to Winchester in the family Ford Cortina, combining a visit to my grandparents with the school prize-giving.

I was ashamed that Norman was training to be a minister, thinking it the kind of occupation that showed an unstable mind, like believing in fairies. If pressed to tell people what Norman did, I used to stammer that he was a minister. Often that was an end to the questioning, though the mother of one of my friends once asked me which government department he headed.

In Edinburgh, I had the freedom to walk around the city centre on my own and discovered the novelty of shopping, an experience made possible by my parents' decision to give me pocket money of ten shillings a week. To encourage thrift, only five shillings was handed over, the remaining five being credited in a small red book so that I could save it to buy something special. It sounded sensible but as 'something special' was not defined, I was to discover that releasing the funds was not straightforward.

The two shops I had a particular fondness for were Boots, where I bought records and Woolworths where I bought tools. The precision of tools gave them an appeal distinct from any utility they possessed. As they were surprisingly cheap, I began to collect them, in the process developing a quite unjustified reputation in the family for being practical.

The freedom of the holidays was spoiled only by the inevitable dental appointment. I knew Nancie would make one without fail and would open her diary with dread to find the date.

Our dentist was working out his final years before retirement. Most of his patients, including my grandparents, were private but we came for free National Health treatment. A slight man, he bent forward as he peered at my mouth, working his way round my teeth with his quisling probe. He wore dark suit trousers and a starched white tunic which with his half-moon spectacles gave him the look of a Nazi doctor, an image I was happy to foster.

My experience of dentists had not been good. As a child of five, I had received my first filling, given without anaesthetic. As the drill danced on the nerves of my tooth, tears ran down my cheeks, while the dentist kept repeating, in defiance of what she was observing, that Scotsmen never cry.

In the days leading up to dental appointments, I would build myself up into hysteria, whining and crying in an unpleasant way. Once Nancie snapped and told me that compared with the pain Deborah had endured without complaint, going to the dentist was nothing. Though my moaning did not stop, the reproach reduced it from a flood to a sullen dribble.

I was taken to dentists with dismaying regularity, as my teeth were crowded and irregular. Most of them were thoroughly drilled and filled – usually without anaesthetic.

My parents too had poor teeth and even while still in their forties had a significant number of false teeth on plates that they took out and put in a glass overnight. On television there were advertisements for false teeth cleaners that fizzed in the glass, so they were not alone.

And then there was sex. Neither of my parents was puritanical about the subject. When Nancie had sat on the edge of the bed and given me a talk that I had found useful, she had been honest and calm. But she felt it important that sex should take place within the context of marriage and was inclined to dismiss any more frivolous aspect of it as being 'unnecessary', pronouncing the word as if to imply that it was also an unwanted burden. I silently disagreed because unnecessary sex was about the only thing I ever thought about.

Onanism aside, the other way I abused my body was that I bit my nails very badly indeed. In despair, my parents promised me a transistor radio if I grew my nails during the summer holidays.

A radio was a powerful incentive, especially a transistor radio which did not need to be plugged into an electrical socket. Somewhat to my surprise, I won the bet and was given a small brown Philips model with an earpiece. My parents were upset when I started the nail-biting again after returning to school but at least I knew that I could stop if I wanted to, so the bribe was not in vain.

Now that I had my radio, I could listen to Radio Luxembourg on 208 metres on the Medium Wave Band. The reception was poor, but it gave me access to pop music which at the time was disdained by the BBC, apart from its broadcast once a week of the top twenty best-selling pop records.

Listening to Pick of the Pops on the BBC was an unbreakable weekly ritual. Norman had bought a reel-to-reel tape recorder to help him master Hebrew at theological college, but was content for Alasdair and me to use it to record the Top 20, which we did by placing a microphone in front of the transistor radio. It was a crude arrangement, requiring us to remain silent or be out of the room for the duration of the recording, but it meant we could replay the songs during the week. If we liked any of them sufficiently well, we would buy a single from Boots for 6/8d, a price that stood as firmly as the Rock of Gibraltar.

Around this time, I was aware that there was something going on in the world that was dangerous and involved the Russians and the Americans. I watched President Kennedy making the speech in Berlin when to universal acclaim he announced that he was a doughnut, though I doubt that I saw it live as I will have been at school.

When I heard of Kennedy's assassination, I was at school standing in the corridor outside my dormitory, wearing my pyjamas and dressing gown, waiting for my turn to have a bath. A boy came up to me and asked me if I had heard the news. Not having heard any news, I asked him if it was the same news that I had heard. He cupped his hands and whispered in my ear that President Kennedy had been shot. I nodded solemnly and said it was the same news I had heard. Earlier that evening we had been learning to sing 'The Cowboy Carol', which had the lines 'There'll be a brand new way of livin' that'll sweep like lightnin' fire and take away the hate from every land.' For the next few days, the tune and those words played on loop in my head.

Aware that life in a basement flat would be constraining for Alasdair and me, some friends who owned a market garden lent my parents their luxurious house on their estate in East Lothian for two weeks.

For the first few days Alasdair and I explored on bikes, but then we were introduced to two girls of about our age from the nearby village of East Linton, who came up to ride a pony which was kept in a field by the house. They taught us to canter and gallop and took us in a pony and trap round the local roads. By doing things together, we got to know them. It was my first natural encounter with girls. I was sorry when we had to leave.

My parents had always enjoyed their social life, though now they had to organise parties without the assistance of servants. If they were the hosts, it was Norman's role to go to the grocer in Stockbridge where a man wearing a brown overall would sell him Hungarian wine. I suspect the choice was dictated by economy more than palate, as he spoke wistfully of the Gevrey-Chambertin he used to drink while at Cambridge in a tone that acknowledged it had now become a taste beyond reach.

In addition to providing the wine, Norman, a lifelong non-smoker, was also responsible for the provision of cigarettes. If he knew some of his guests were smokers, he would make sure the silver cigarette boxes, given to him as leaving presents when moving from one job to another in the Burmah Oil Company, were full. The exercise was as pointless as it was wasteful. I often handed round the boxes and found that most people said they preferred to smoke their own, the men patting the inside pockets of their jackets and the women their handbags to give me reassurance about the adequacy of their supply. As a result, most of our cigarettes remained unsmoked, became stale and were thrown away.

Nancie's role in the giving of dinner parties was more straightforward as she was only required to choose the menu, order the ingredients for delivery, cook the food, lay the table, serve the food and wash up.

Money must have been tight for my parents as they had no income and were paying out money for school fees and living expenses at a considerable rate. From time to time Norman had a bout of what he called 'financial indigestion' and it was one of these that was to cause a significant change in the direction of my life.

One afternoon the headmaster came up to me and said he had had a letter from a day school in Edinburgh asking if I was interested in taking up a place. He wanted to know if he should throw it in the bin. I told him not to.

Some months earlier, during the holidays, Norman had just returned from bidding for a desk at an auction sale and we were trying to lift it into the house from the basement area. As we paused to take breath, he told me I needed to work harder so that, like Alasdair, I could try for a scholarship at Fettes College. He was convinced I was able enough but felt I was held back by idleness.

To emphasise his message further, Norman said he was unsure that they would be able to pay the full school fees for Fettes and that I might have to go to a local school if I failed to get the scholarship, and as there were few grammar schools left, it would have to be a secondary modern. When I asked what that was, he just shook his head and said I would not want to go to one.

At this point we might have moved the desk into the house and our conversation would have been forgotten, but Norman added that he had paid five pounds to have me registered for a private day school in Edinburgh and for some reason I thought that significant.

When the headmaster spoke to me about the offer from the day school, he assumed I wanted him to decline it, but in my twelve-year-old mind I thought I shouldn't waste five pounds without asking my parents first.

While waiting for an answer from home, I began to think about my options and decided it was lower risk to go to the day school as an ordinary pupil than to sit a scholarship exam for Fettes and fail. Such lack of ambition would be hard to sell to my parents, so I told them that I wanted to make my own reputation, free from Alasdair's shadow. The reasoning was not only understood, it was applauded. I even began to believe it.

In my final days at prep school, I had to go through one last ritual, which was to receive a talk about sex from the headmaster, given to all leavers individually in his study.

He was relaxed and as usual was smoking a cigarette when I went in. By his desk a large wooden radio was crooning muffled light music to cover the discussion from any eavesdropper listening from the library next door.

The talk drifted from subject to subject as if he were a guide in a country house, inviting me to take notice of objects of interest as they caught his attention. We started with the act itself, though to my disappointment he failed to advance my state of knowledge, saying only that a man put his P into a woman, something I already knew. What I wanted to know was how the docking procedure took place but there was no clarification about that.

We moved on to talk about feelings. I should bear in mind that women sometimes didn't want to do it as much as men did, and that I should be sensitive in that direction, even on my wedding night. Then he threw in some biological facts before warning me in an oblique way of the dangers lurking in dormitories, something I was already aware of but would be protected from at a day school.

Soon I realised that I was not going to be told anything useful and was starting to lose interest. I was jolted back to attention when he asked me what the Latin words 'contra' and 'incipio' meant. I had been forewarned by another boy that this question would be put so knew the answer, which led him neatly into a description of how to have sex without having babies. Again, I learned nothing new as I already knew about FLs and the newspapers were filled with debate about the contraceptive pill. I left the room disappointed.

My parents drove down from Scotland for my final prize-giving at prep school, a trip which nearly ended in tragedy. Following their practice of driving through the night to avoid traffic congestion, they had just passed Oxford when at three o'clock in the morning Nancie had fallen asleep at the wheel. The car left the road and crashed into a telegraph pole. Fortunately, they were both wearing safety belts and survived unscathed but for bruised shoulders, so I was spared the fate I had witnessed of boys being taken out of class by a sombre headmaster, only to return a few minutes later, crying. Routine was never broken for grief. The silver lining of the crash was that we travelled to Edinburgh by train.

CHAPTER 6

Day School

In 1965, Norman had been inducted as a minister in a coalmining town and we were living in a manse that overlooked the River Forth. The house was perched on levelled ground, halfway up a steep hill on the east side of the town, and was surrounded on all sides by fields. Its appeal to me was its size. If I counted a dressing room and a large cloak room, I could boast fourteen rooms and two bathrooms. The disadvantage was that it was cold, even in summer, as the builder had designed it for the view to the north and the sun only shone through the frosted panes of the bathroom and toilet windows.

We had moved into the house at the end of the summer. The furnishing was a mixture of styles, nearly everything, including beds and carpets, bought second or third hand in Edinburgh auction sales. Norman had a good eye for furniture, but he also had a budget. Harmony was rare and coincidental. My own room, two floors up at the top of the house, gave me space and privacy.

Far away, at the other end of town, was the colliery. The slag heap and colliery hoist loomed over the surrounding area which was itself as desolate as a railway goods yard. Its influence seeped into every part of the community. Years of free coal, burned in the fireplaces of the terraced houses, had blackened every stone. Not even the large houses, built for the affluent high up on the ridge to catch the wind and gain the view, had escaped the invisible particles that in places had built up imperceptibly into a coat of solid black.

Mining was the main employment for men, but it was not their only option for manual work. Near the centre of the town was an iron foundry where workers sweated over the production of anything that could be cast, including the manhole covers that spread the town's name throughout the country. The work there was also hot and hard, though those who toiled there could at least see the sun and the sky.

Both jobs were physically demanding and dangerous, the shared risk being the blood that bound them. The hazard of unfenced mechanical equipment or molten iron might be obvious, but it was harder to appreciate that dust and fumes settled in pink lungs, biding their time.

Few jobs were done by both men and women. For the most part women who left school without qualifications worked in shops, the laundrette or as low-grade administrative staff. Some were employed in a factory on the east side of town that made shirts under contract for the retail chain, Marks & Spencer. Accurately anticipating the impact of globalisation, Marks & Spencer had all their clothing made in the UK, explaining that if they did not, they would have no customers who could afford to buy their products.

The most popular job for women was on the labelling line at the VAT 69 bottling plant in South Queensferry, a half-hour bus journey away. It involved nothing more than applying labels to bottles but the action could be done in an automatic state, allowing the mind to drift.

Away from the pit and iron foundry, there was another side to the town. Miners and foundry workers earned some of the highest wages paid for manual work. Feeding on their efforts were all the support services that kept people clothed, fed, healthy and entertained. Few, if any, became rich, but compared with the two decades of rationing and shortage that people had lived through so recently, it was a time of milk and honey.

The centre of town reflected a community in balance. Though aesthetically barren, on a Saturday morning it was busy with people standing in queues outside shops as they waited to be served and caught up with the craic.

The council houses in which most of the workers lived, allowed a life of self-respect and security. Though often clad in drab brown pebbledash, they were for the most part generously built on large plots that were tended with pride. Others, the products of a rushed post-war building programme, had been constructed cheaply, and though only a decade old, had an air of desolation, with damp patches on their walls and flaking paint. Wherever they lived, people knew each other from the social club, the pub or the church. When the pit and foundry closed in the summer, the workers often went on holiday together.

In the centre of town, there were two cinemas, where children would be sent on a Saturday afternoon to give their parents peace. Uninterested in the film, the children would talk loudly and fool around in the cheap seats in the front of the stalls, while the usherettes flashed their torches along the rows of seats to shame them into keeping quiet. As a last resort, the film would be stopped until silence, or at least a reasonable approximation of silence, was restored. At a showing of *The Great Escape* that I watched from the safety of the circle, the prisoners of war had their incarceration extended while the film was paused no fewer than three times.

It was an unfamiliar experience being a dayboy at school. The countdown to the end of the school holidays was free from the regret of parting. No longer was the last week of the holidays spent calculating first the days and then the hours until I had to leave home. Instead, school seemed little more than an unwanted interruption to a life of agreeable idleness. The drawback was that the end of term had a greatly reduced excitement.

In the mornings, Norman always made me a boiled egg and toast which I would eat while listening to the *Today* programme. The presenter, Jack de Manio, brought a reassuring amateurism to the broadcast. Famously he could never tell the time, usually getting the hour wrong and often giving up altogether, as if overwhelmed by the task. As people still wore mechanical watches of unreliable accuracy, one of the programme's purposes was to give regular and accurate time checks, so his failure was a serious one. He had an endearing habit of arriving at the BBC studio in his Rolls Royce motor car while wearing his pyjamas and dressing gown, as if protesting that the hours that he was expected to work were demeaning to someone of his importance.

It was on the *Today* programme that I heard a news item announcing breathlessly that a house in London had sold for over a hundred thousand pounds. The nation gasped in unison.

After breakfast I would walk a hundred yards up the hill to the bus stop where the green SMT bus was due at ten past eight. If I was late, I would end up racing the bus with my arm outstretched, pleading for it to stop, which it mostly did. The door would fold open and I would clamber aboard into a wall of smoke.

Almost everybody on the bus smoked. Even the driver smoked as he drove, skilfully flicking the pack open and tapping it on a hard surface to make a cigarette rise up so that he could extract it with his lips, ready to light. The bus conductors too would jam a cigarette in their mouths, leaving their hands free to take money, adjust the heavy ticket machines that hung on a leather strap round their necks, and whirl the handle that produced the ticket.

The bus was usually nearly full. Many of the passengers were women, going to factory production lines or to offices where they worked as secretaries or administrative assistants. It might have taken forty-five minutes to get to Edinburgh, but it was a precious forty-five minutes on their own.

I was conspicuous in my school uniform, especially my cap which stood out like a provocation, state schools in the area having abandoned the wearing of them. Most of the passengers on the bus would have known that I was the minister's son, because they would have seen me coming from the manse every day. Fortunately for me, whatever they might have thought about a boy who had an English accent of such brittleness that only the Queen's strangled vowels could surpass it, they kept it to themselves.

A friend with a flatter English accent than mine was not so lucky when he was sent to the local school where Nancie taught. On his first day, he was called an English bastard and beaten up so badly he had to go home for medical treatment. His parents were missionaries who had just returned from Pakistan. Even at my school, I was mocked for the way I spoke. Whenever I said what I thought was 'Yes', a mocking imitation of 'Nyarz' echoed around the classroom. One morning shortly after I arrived, a boy came up to me, asked me my name and then said I was the new boy everyone was talking about.

Our school was laid out like an army barracks with utilitarian stone-built classrooms set round the perimeter of a tarmac parade ground. In the centre was a Georgian building in the Palladian style which housed the school hall, an oval design of exquisite beauty. Originally standing with the confidence of a country house in open land, the school had been humbled by the construction of houses and tenement flats which now surrounded it, blocking the distant view and reducing it to a number in a suburban street. The final ignominy had been the building of a public washhouse across the road.

My classmates were not unfriendly but most of them had been together throughout their schooling and knew each other and the ways of the school. I was told that the person whose place I had taken had made the all too common flight through the windscreen from the back seat of his mother's car. He had been lucky not to have been killed in the collision, but his brain had been damaged, and he had lost the sight of one eye.

Academically, I did not adjust well in my first year. The class had been doing Science for two years and I found it hard to catch up. Most of the rest of the classes involved learning things by rote and being tested on them, a common pattern of teaching at the time which could make any subject dull. It was like being taught to ski by having to learn the heights of all the surrounding mountains. A great deal of emphasis was placed on copying neatly into exercise books what was written on blackboards. As my writing verged on being illegible, I did not excel.

One master, who was overweight, was bullied by the boys and frequently reduced to tears. His inability to keep control of a class should have led to his dismissal, if only to encourage him to find a job he would have enjoyed more. Other masters used to hear the noise and come into the class to check that he was all right. His failure must have been widely known in the common room, yet nothing was done. We learned little from him and the lessons were an embarrassment.

Another sad fact was that for me girls remained firmly untouchable in their parallel railway carriage. I was tormented every morning when our bus stopped for a girl of extraordinary beauty, who went to our sister school in Edinburgh. Her uniform fitted as if made by a French couturier. I was dazzled but had no idea how to speak to her or make contact. Someone who knew her told me that her character was as beautiful as her looks, which only made my suffering worse. I hoped she might sit next to me and that we might talk, but she never did.

Sport is often thought to take boys' minds off sex, which it does effectively but only for the duration of the game. We played rugby in the winter and Easter terms, though many of the boys would have preferred to play football. Whereas at boarding school, my kit had been hung up to dry in the changing rooms and then washed according to a rota, at day school I had to look after it myself. Being lazy, I jammed my rugby strip into a duffel bag and left it there until the next game, sweaty, muddy and wet. We were supposed to have clean kit for matches on Saturday mornings which meant begging Nancie to wash it on a Friday, something I occasionally remembered to do.

In my first Easter holidays, my parents paid for me to go on a school holiday to Paris and Avignon, a kind gesture on their part to help me build friendships. It was the first time I had been to continental Europe other than to touch down briefly in sterile airports and sit in cafeterias waiting for refuelling to be completed and technical hitches to be fixed.

Arriving in France, we walked down the gangway from the ferry and climbed into the railway carriages. Everything felt different. The loading gauge of the railway was larger than in Britain and the carriages seemed huge, an impression that was heightened by the fact that the platforms were not raised, requiring us to clamber up steps from track level. Inside, the carriage was divided into small compartments entered off a corridor down one side. The flat bench seats were upholstered in practical green leathercloth which on overnight services could, at the pull of various levers, be converted into 'couchette' beds with six beds per compartment.

The hotel in Paris was promisingly named 'Grand Hotel, Paris – Rome', but any grandeur stopped there. It was tucked away up a side street, and the reception desk was presided over by a hag dressed in black, who spent her time scolding us for using the lift, a rickety device with doors of metal parallelograms that had to be pulled open and closed like an accordion.

The hag might have been disagreeable, but she knew how to maximise the financial return from her assets. To get to the bedroom that I shared with two others, I had first to go through another bedroom with three beds side by side. These filled the room as completely as a double bed in a camper van, with no gap between them, leaving only a passageway about two feet wide at the foot of the beds, which led to the bathroom. At the other side of the bathroom was an open doorway which was the entrance to our room. The door itself had been taken off the hinges because there was no room to open it. We did not even have space to walk at the foot of our beds, as they fitted the area of the floor exactly. Instead we had to throw our cases onto the beds and scramble after them. As the bathroom had been turned into a corridor, we used it only for brushing our teeth.

After two days of visiting the tourist sights, we caught the night train south, sleeping on the couchette beds.

In Avignon, we stayed in a convent, a simple building with twin-bedded rooms, either side of a long corridor. We were allowed to wander the town on our own, going out at night to circus stalls to have our money teased away from us by stallholders coaxing us to play games of skill in the hope of winning bottles of cheap sparkling wine.

I bought my first ever bottle of wine from a small wine merchant, who was unconcerned about selling alcohol to a thirteen-year-old boy, though he warned me of its possible effects by touching his head. He must have believed my story that I was buying it as a present for my father because he sold me a bottle of Chateauneuf-du-Pape, Domaine de la Solitude, which was far above the normal price range for teenage drinking. I kept the bottle as a table light after we had drunk it in celebration of Norman's birthday and remember vividly the three bees on the label.

On the way home, we lost one of the boys on the train from Paris to Calais. He eventually re-joined the group, having caught another train. The incident will have caused the teachers an hour or two of anxiety, but it ended well and was forgotten. The boy himself seemed not in the slightest put out.

In the summer term we played cricket, but it was not a game that felt comfortable in Edinburgh at a day school. There were no lazy afternoons in the heat, with games drifting on until late afternoon with long shadows. Instead we arrived in the grey of a cool Saturday morning, often playing in drizzle with fewer than eleven players, most of whom would rather have been playing football. After the collapse of both side's batting, we would make our way back home in time for a late lunch, indifferent to the result of the game.

At the end of my first year at the school, we went for a family camping holiday near Aviemore. On our return, my first action on entering the house was to pick up the pile of mail that lay on the doormat at the back door and find the envelope containing my school report. After locking myself in the bathroom I opened it and, as I read it, my eyes welled up with tears. I hid it in my bedroom and later burned it.

My parents mentioned that it was strange that they had not received a report. I worried that they might contact the school, but they never did. Besides, in the days of pen and ink, once something was gone, it was gone. In retrospect it was the most foolish action I could have taken, because it denied me access to help, but at the time I felt deeply ashamed.

The next year was little more successful than the first. The two subjects I enjoyed most were art and music – art because it gave me a grounding in the styles of the best-known painters and music because it made me realise that classical music was not a yoke to be born with stoicism. The first time I heard *Carmina Burana* I was so excited that it had no boring sections and consisted only of climaxes that I rushed out and bought a budget recording, which I played endlessly in my room through a loudspeaker mounted in a box covered in wood-grained Fablon. I only learned later that the Nazis were also excited by the music for similar reasons.

Girls remained out of reach, though sometimes they would come into my life for a tantalising moment. In the summer holidays, shortly before I was fifteen, we travelled south to see my grandparents in Lymington and visited friends from Burmah Oil days. They had a daughter who was vivacious and pretty. I loved talking to her over lunch and was sad when we left, knowing that I would never find anyone remotely like her in the town where we lived.

I enjoyed living at home, particularly because I grew to know my parents well. Norman was helpful in the way he passed on wisdom, frequently talking about problems that arose in the parish, though in a way that protected anonymity. The scales fell from my eyes when he told me how common incest was in the community. It was something that seemed to me to be so hideous that it must exist only in theory, but he said in a deliberately off-hand way that for many families, a daughter was just another woman for the father.

On Saturday lunchtimes if I wasn't playing sport, I helped him distribute Meals on Wheels to the elderly and saw the houses in which they lived. For the most part they were clean and decent, though they often had a smell of talcum powder with hints of incontinence and body odour. The food was plated with an aluminium cover that I would whip off to reveal the beef stew or mince with mashed potatoes and two veg.

On Sundays, I wore a suit and went with Nancie to the eleven o'clock church service. Often there would be several hundred people in the congregation, the men wearing suits and ties, the women in dresses and hats. In the winter many of the women wore fur coats, their thin legs appearing beneath considerable bulk, making them look like sheep. The quality of music was different from that of Winchester Cathedral, the elderly female choir wobbling on notes like a person about to lose their balance. Nancie used to take exception to the fact that the congregation could not keep up with the organ and, as if to lead her troops up to the enemy pillbox, used to outpace the organ and then in a stage whisper mutter 'Dragging! Dragging!' while waiting for everyone to catch up.

Nancie taught me the basics of cooking, though it was hard to make anything well because the gas cooker had endless faults, any one of which should have been enough to ensure that it was taken to the dump. The gas taps controlling the hob had become stiff and the plastic covers had sheared off, with the result that they could only be turned with an adjustable spanner. The grill had heat-reflecting plates that fell into the food in the grill pan and were too hot to remove, and the oven had a broken thermostat that resulted in it overheating. A less important failure was that the complex mechanical automatic timer for the oven had also broken, though it is probable that its workings had never been understood.

I gave up cooking in fury when a stew I made to an Elizabeth David recipe burned to a crisp after I had left it to cook during the Sunday church service, despite the flame being adjusted to the lowest setting and the pan being placed on an asbestos heat disperser, but Nancie persevered in a way that I now regard as saintly.

The replacement of the cooker remained an unshifting item on the agenda for discussion with the Kirk Session, the church body responsible for the fittings of the house. Norman felt awkward making the request because it never seemed to be the right year in which to incur the expense. Why he did not go out and buy one himself remained a mystery. We were not destitute.

Norman's delinquency in the kitchen extended beyond a lack of care for the equipment. He would from time to time help with the washing up but would leave to soak anything that offered even a modest challenge, such as the milk pan from his morning coffee. Our lack of consideration typically reached its zenith on a Thursday when Nancie, after a full day's work at school and an evening of cooking at home, went out to the Women's Guild. Frequently she would return to find the washing up still undone. Norman and I would exchange nervous glances as she crashed pots. When it was safe to speak, we would wonder why she was being so unreasonably bad tempered.

If my own performance in the kitchen was not a great deal better than Norman's, my defence was that I found Nancie's untidiness hard to live with. She belonged to the school of thought that everything should be at hand so that it would be there when you needed it. As a result, much of the precious work surface was covered with jars, bottles and utensils which, like magnets, attracted other objects. An aunt once observed drolly after doing the washing up, that it was impossible to know if she had finished because the normal sign of a clear surface did not exist. I once made the mistake of trying to persuade Nancie to keep out only the things she needed regularly, but gave up when every suggestion received the reply, 'You'd be surprised how often I use that.'

As if Nancie's life was not hard enough, Lizzie and Douglas came to live with us when they were both in their early nineties and no longer able to look after themselves. We gave them a large bedroom on the east side of the house, from where as they sat in their wing-backed chairs they had a view to the east, towards the Forth Bridges.

Lizzie maintained her correspondence, writing in small spidery writing on a table that could be slid in from the side of her chair. Douglas was by this time 'wandered' though he was always cheerful and looked through his small tin trunk reading sermons he had given. To the irritation of Nancie, he often came down an hour or so before supper, offering to help. In despair, she left a note at the bottom of the stairs saying 'HDS go back to your room'. Surprisingly it worked, as he always recognised his initials and did as instructed, with the result that the stairs creaked as he went up and down like a perpetual motion machine. He was appreciative of his meals and frequently remarked how good the hotel was, sometimes tipping Nancie a penny.

One evening there was a crash and Nancie discovered Douglas lying at the foot of the stairs. As she approached, he said that he was going 'to a higher place'. With tears in her eyes, she held his hand as he died – except he didn't. After a few minutes of holding the tableau, Douglas began to fret and, seeking a way of breaking the impasse, felt in his pocket for a Hawick Ball, a large spherical sweet, which he popped into his mouth. It was not the action of a dying man. Nancie helped him to his feet and he climbed ponderously up the stairs to his stated destination.

Douglas and Lizzie sat in silence most of the day, having long since decided that television held no pleasure. In Balerno, they had had a valve wireless, but my grandfather had insisted that it ran on gas and refused to bring it when they moved as they had no gas supply in the bedroom. We offered them a modern radio, but they had showed no interest. Their lack of technical sophistication proved an unexpected problem when Norman went to a conference in Newfoundland and Lizzie became hostile to Nancie, asking her who the man was in the house late at night and in the early morning. Nancie was mystified until she realised it was the voice of Radio 4.

On Sundays we laboriously gathered up Douglas and Lizzie and drove them down to church. After one of the services Douglas announced to Nancie that the man who had given the sermon was a very great friend of his. Nancie replied brightly that that was a lovely comment as the man was his son. Douglas wasn't accepting that and, drawing on the full strength of a Northern Irishman's indignation, said that he had never done anything to any young girl that would have resulted in her having a baby.

Lizzie died aged ninety-six and Douglas aged a hundred. He had spent the last years of his life in a nursing home. On his last birthday, he was thrilled to receive a letter of congratulations from the Queen, saying he had only met her on one occasion and never thought that she would remember him.

My academic performance through the school remained pedestrian, though I was always in the top sets for most subjects. Reluctantly, having never caught up with the class, I abandoned Science after only three years and concentrated on English, French, History and Latin.

I was not disciplined about doing my homework. On the way home from school, I would settle into a seat at the bus terminus at St Andrew Square and think about doing my homework, though only for a second before reaching for a copy of *Autocar or Motor* that I had bought from the news stand. Once at home, I would change out of my school uniform and go upstairs to my bedroom, ostensibly to do my homework, before eventually receiving a call via the intercom to come down for supper. Any enquiry from my parents about homework would be parried with a grunt. If I had to write something out, I might do the work, but if it was a question of reading a passage in a book or learning vocabulary, I would leave it for the bus journey in the morning. On the bus journey, I would run out of time.

In the summer of 1968, we went on a package holiday to Mutters in the Austrian Alps, a place chosen by Norman because my parents spoke German and the walking was good, his two requirements.

In school uniform, immaculately turned out for a passport photograph.

Government restrictions on buying foreign exchange were still in place and in the week before leaving, Norman took our passports to the bank so that they could be marked up with the amount of sterling he had used to buy travellers' cheques in Austrian schillings. Fortunately, the annual allowance of fifty pounds each was more than enough for our needs.

Most people took travellers' cheques or cash, as credit cards were not yet widely known about, far less accepted, either in Britain or on the Continent. The concept of spending someone else's money had yet to be understood.

Travellers' cheques were issued in set amounts like large bank notes. Immediately you received them, you signed them. When you came to cash them, either at a hotel, a shop or a bank, you signed them again and the signature was confirmed against the one you had signed on issue and the one in your passport.

On the journey out, we spent two nights in the Regent Palace Hotel in Soho so that we could see some of the sights of London and meet friends. Our MP, Tam Dalyell, took us round the House of Commons. Tam lived close to us and he and Kathleen had been to our house for dinner on a number of occasions. My parents admired them both.

As Tam showed us the offices, he talked of the stress imposed on marriages by the job of being an MP. While some marriages failed as a result of traditional infidelity, many dissolved over time because the wife living in the constituency envied the close working relationship between the MP and his secretary: most MPs were men. It didn't matter that their behaviour was beyond reproach; it was enough that when the MP's wife phoned the secretary she felt like a supplicant.

We took the boat train from Victoria to Folkestone and crossed by ferry to Calais. The couchette to Innsbruck was overheated. I was thirsty but as we couldn't buy any drinking water, I resorted to drinking the red wine that came with my tray of dinner, which only made my thirst greater. As a result I slept badly.

We were driven up to our resort in a Mercedes-Benz taxi arranged by the travel company which had organised the package tour. Apart from the Bentley, it was quieter and smoother than any car I had ever been in, its gears changing magically by themselves as we swept our way up the curving mountain road.

I knew all about Austria because I had seen the film of *The Sound of Music* no fewer than three times at the Edinburgh Odeon. Each time I sat back in the red plush seats of the cinema, I knew with an adopted child's certainty of its noble birth, that I could be one of the children and be loved by Julie Andrews. They would never notice another child in the line-up: they had so many, they probably never even counted them.

I was less certain about Christopher Plummer, who looked more like a man who had just brought his new Jag back from the golf course than an admiral in the Austrian navy. It didn't help that he had been given lines so wooden that it was unlikely that the words would have flowed naturally from any human being. But the complaint was trivial. I loved the film and if it was thought by some to be cloyingly oversentimental, I licked up every drop of honey.

The Austrian scenery turned out to be exactly as I expected, the houses and landscape appearing to be the creation of a single mind. The grass was as lush and uniformly green as a billiard table. The houses were made from local wood and white-painted breeze block, their dark roofs spread like tented sheets pulled taut in shallow vees to overhang balconies and walls in protection against rain and snow. On some of the houses, murals had been painted to embellish windows or depict a country or religious scene and from all, geraniums cascaded from unseen flower boxes. At the back of the houses, men cut wood to a measured length and split it with an axe before stacking it in piles as neatly as cigarettes in a pack.

All this was the product of an ordered society where individuality had been willingly surrendered to build a brand of which people were proud. There were no cars propped up on bricks, waiting to be restored at a time that would never come. There were no garden sheds cheaply erected and in varying stages of dilapidation, sitting incongruously large on small plots. There were no weeds or self-sown shrubs or brambles. There was no fencing made from old planks, corrugated iron and barbed wire. There were no fridges or washing machines moved from the house to be taken to the dump and then quietly forgotten deep at the end of the garden. No caravans sat on driveways, their cream paint mottled with lichen. No builders had put up houses of defiant ugliness. In short there was none of the rebelliousness of a British village.

For us, the perfection of Austria was a strong part of its charm. We had long walks, ate picnics prepared by the hotel and sat down every night to our table d'hôte menu, the only decision being whether or not my parents could justify the expense of ordering hock. Alasdair and I shared a bedroom which had the rare luxury of an ensuite shower and the even greater luxury of a feather bag on the bed, later to be reintroduced to us by Habitat as the duvet.

We had signed up for a number of excursions, driving in pouring rain to Salzburg where Mozart had been elbowed out by the Family von Trapp as if he were some elderly relative who had become a bore. We made up for it in part by visiting his birthplace in Innsbruck, but then betrayed him by going to a concert to hear Beethoven's Fifth Symphony.

On returning home to Scotland, we prepared to receive two teenage boys who were to be billeted on us under an exchange scheme with some towns in New England. Called 'Operation Friendship', it was set up by an American minister who was working in Scotland and had the simple purpose of bringing together people from different countries, in the idealistic post-war vision of a world in which experience would temper prejudice. Our town had been paired with one in Massachusetts and we were hosting twenty teenagers in families for three weeks.

When we gathered for the first time, the Americans seemed noticeably different from ourselves, being taller, healthier, better dressed and more confident.

Their confidence was at times overwhelming. They viewed the fridge, not as a safe from which food and drink would be withdrawn by us as their hosts, but as a water fountain to which they could go when they felt the need. They wore their trousers once and then gave them to Nancie to wash; and they asked to use the telephone in the morning when it was charged at peak rate. But all these were but pinpricks compared with their profligate use of the bath which they would run as casually as we might fill a basin to wash our hands. Any British child knew not to accept the offer of a bath in someone else's house. Obviously, over a period of three weeks, baths would need to be taken, but that would be a matter of polite negotiation and the timing would have to be planned with care.

I subsequently discovered that in their briefing before coming to Scotland, our guests had been told that a tin bath would be brought out and placed in the living room in front of the fire and would be filled with water heated on a stove. As guests, they would be offered first use before the family followed. They had possibly been so thrilled by the prospect of not having to navigate the etiquette of such a situation that they had been lulled into thinking that our domestic plumbing was as advanced as theirs.

Over the following weeks we drove our guests round the country, sometimes going to plenary events with other towns and their guests. One of these was held at an outdoor training centre in Aberfoyle, a village in the hills to the east of Loch Lomond. The speaker of honour was Wendy Wood, a founder of the National Party of Scotland which later became the Scottish National Party. Naturally she spoke about the case for Scottish independence from the United Kingdom. Her economic argument relied heavily on trees. Norway had trees and was an independent country. Scotland had trees too.

For nearly an hour, she denigrated the English, using exaggerated accents to caricature them and describing their appalling behaviour over recent centuries. It was hardly in the spirit of international friendship, but the organisers were content that she had given the American guests an idea of Scotland's frustration and ambition.

At the end of her talk, I heard the Americans reflecting on the dreadfulness of the English and felt indignant that Wendy Wood had been chosen to address us. I might have felt less badly had I known that she herself was born English. Fortunately, the Warsaw Pact countries had invaded Czechoslovakia the previous night and, as the news trickled through, everyone quickly became distracted by the thought of a European war.

We spent many evenings singing Scottish folk songs and drinking Tennant's lager as we formed a strong bond. The Americans couldn't recognise the signals of our class system

OPERATION 1968 FRIENDSHIP

ABERFOYLE SCOTLAND

nor we theirs, so each group defined the other as classless and formed friendships without inhibition.

The highlight of their trip was a visit down the pit of the working colliery. It was confined to the boys, the practical reason being that we had to join the men in the communal showers to clean the coal dust off at the end of the visit. We descended for a long time in a caged lift and then walked along roadways under the River Forth, keeping clear of the rails for the wheeled wagons or 'bogies' that brought the coal from the face. I remember only the darkness, the heat and the feeling of danger, but I learned enough on that trip to understand why Tam Dalyell, in defiance of all electoral good sense, tried to hasten the end of the coal industry.

In July the following year we travelled to Southbridge, Massachusetts. Each person had earned fifty pounds to put towards the costs, with the balance raised through communal activities. My contribution to the sale of work was to have made some wooden wheelbarrows using plywood that was supplied to me by the adult in charge of the project but, having neither instructions, nor a workbench, nor the correct tools, nor wheels, I never completed the task. Eventually, after keeping the man at bay for many months by making vague promises and dodging direct questions, I confessed I had not made them. He looked despairing as he took away his bits of wood, but I was relieved. The commitment had been made without consulting me and the task was beyond my skill.

We flew to New York on a Pan-Am charter flight from Prestwick Airport. Regular air fares were still high and charter flights were the only way of obtaining a cheap ticket. For most of the people in our group, it was the first time they had ever flown.

The dinner tray had a complimentary pack of three cigarettes which I kept as a souvenir, until curiosity got the better of me some months later and I tried to smoke one. The main course was Beef Stroganoff and must have been finished off in the galley, because some of the girls from our town said in horrified tones that they had seen the stewardesses putting sour cream into it. The words 'sour cream' rippled down the cabin like a rumour in wartime, with the result that many people refused to touch the food, as if someone was trying to make them ill. Alasdair and I gorged on it.

There were thunderstorms over New York which prevented us from landing there and we were diverted to Bangor in Maine where it was hot and humid. The captain tried to arrange for the aircraft to be hooked up to an air-conditioning unit, but none was available. As a result, we were left to swelter. To compensate us for our suffering, they served Moët et Chandon champagne on the final leg. I was only fifteen, but as I was one of the few people still awake, the stewardesses kept refilling my glass and I drank a great deal of it, the taste fixing in my head as securely as the news of Kennedy's assassination had done.

At the airport we were met by a welcoming committee and taken to board a Greyhound bus, its corrugated aluminium body radiating strength and its air-conditioning soothing us back to the climate we had so recently left. We stepped aboard in the darkness and sank into its comfortable seats for the three-hour journey down the turnpike.

The following morning, I felt like Alice; everything was bigger and better, especially the colour television that ran all day, often showing David Frost who by then was commuting weekly to New York with his notepad. I felt proud that British intellect was so obviously superior that it was worth the cost of a weekly First Class return ticket from London. Seeing him in colour, albeit with a purple tinge, was very exciting indeed.

When we gathered for our first group session, the impression I had drawn the previous year about Americans' looks was confirmed. A number of the girls, new to the enlarged group, were almost of pre-Raphaelite beauty.

The formula of being with a family and doing normal things, interspersed with special trips, avoided the ennui of inactivity or the tedium of relentless sight-seeing. Over the next few weeks, we swam in lakes, had a clam bake at Cape Cod, went to New York, visited a re-created village at Old

Sturbridge, had a day trip to Boston and stayed with host families in New Hampshire. It was thrilling to be abroad without my parents, a feeling of independence reinforced by my sixteen-year-old host who was licensed to drive and owned a new Corvair convertible with a radio. With the roof down and the radio playing 'In the Year 2525', seemingly on loop in between urgent and compelling advertisements, the blood surged.

The visit to New York was a turning point in my life. It was not the Statue of Liberty that did it, nor the Rockefeller Centre, nor the United Nations Building, nor even the Rockettes and the showing of *True Grit* at Radio City. It was a beautiful dark-haired girl – tall, skinny and flat chested – who sat next to me on the three-hour journey home and kissed me the entire way. I was now inside the railway carriage but had no idea how I had got there.

To my delight, I discovered that she had plans for how we might spend evenings when we were not obliged to go to group functions. She would meet me after supper in her father's Pontiac Bonneville which had an enormous front bench seat, and we would glide out into a wood where she would park in a clearing littered with Budweiser beer cans. There was a curfew agreed by the host parents, requiring us all to be back with our families by ten o'clock at night, so time was limited. Fortunately, she didn't waste time and started to kiss from the moment the engine was switched off. All we did was kiss, but to a fifteen-year-old boy who had hardly spent a moment with a girl in his life, it was incredibly exciting.

The kissing continued every time we were on a Greyhound bus. We kissed to Cape Cod, we kissed to Boston and we kissed to New Hampshire. The kissing started when the bus door shut and it ended when it opened. If I remember little of the journeys, it is because my eyes were closed.

Although for obvious reasons conversation was limited, we managed to talk a little, mostly at her house where we would listen to Judy Collins's album *Wildflowers*, the femininity and wistfulness of the songs amplifying my lovesick yearnings, giving them the illusion of romance.

In between my regular trips in the Pontiac to go kissing, I went to the clearing in the wood on a beer-drinking expedition with the boys. One of the differences between the Americans and ourselves was that we had been drinking alcohol from a pre-pubescent age and were indifferent to it, whereas they were forbidden it and were obsessed by it.

The expedition was planned with melodramatic care. An older boy was to drive to a neighbouring state where, using his brother's ID, he would buy the beer. Once safely back in Massachusetts, he was to have a roadside rendezvous with another boy who would then take half the load in his car to reduce the chance of losing everything to the police, should they decide to do a road check.

It was an absurd amount of work for a drink of beer, but the plan went smoothly and in due course we arrived at the clearing after supper and solemnly drank beer by the light of the car headlights. It was a dull ritual, done to make a point and not for pleasure. The only interest was watching a boy drinking a can in a few seconds, a feat so astonishing it appeared an illusion, accomplished by piercing a hole in the base of the can which he put to his lips while opening his throat and pulling the ring pull.

When we came to drive home, one of the cars failed to start, the drain from the headlamps too much for the battery. Nothing is more dead than a full-sized American car with power steering and automatic transmission without a turning engine. There was no option but to leave it where it was and go back for it the following day. Naturally the parents of the boy whose car had been left behind were suspicious and the father came out with us to retrieve it. With extraordinary perspicacity he looked at the car, axle deep in empty beer cans and announced that there must have been liquor drinking. To everyone's astonishment, the car started first time, the battery having recovered charge overnight. If there were reprisals for the episode, we were never told of them.

On 24 July, towards the end of our exchange, Neil Armstrong landed on the moon. Unlike the assassination of President Kennedy or the destruction of the Twin Towers, I cannot remember where I was as I followed its descent on television. Had the mission failed, I would have remembered every detail, but the landing came at the end of a process that gave the illusion of inevitable success, so I was impatient to see it completed, especially as there were no bright colour images of what was happening. I had become so used to events being filmed from optimal viewpoints that, however much I knew rationally that it was not possible, I still missed not being able to see a shot of the descent filmed in colour from the lunar surface.

As a result of watching the landing, we were late arriving at a barbecue, but thought that the reason would be understood. When I apologised and gave our excuse, the father of the host family said in disgust, 'That's just great!'

Before I could stop myself, I found I had replied, 'Yes it was.' It was an abuse of my position as a guest and the first time I remember being deliberately rude to a stranger, but I felt indignant at his lack of respect for the courage of his countrymen.

During our visit, we became aware of how much the war in Vietnam, a filler on our TV news, was a constant dread for the American boys and for the girls who loved them. When we sang 'Where Have All the Flowers Gone?' we often ended it in tears. If the parents cared, as they must have done, they kept it to themselves. Possibly they were aware that if their son's birthday came up in one of the televised draws for the draft, they would have to be the ones talking calmly of patriotic duty. The safe option was to volunteer for the navy before being drafted. Some of the boys were contemplating it, but many said they preferred to roll the dice.

On our last night before returning to Scotland, we had a party at a private house with the adults on the ground floor and the teenagers in the basement. The adults drank heavily as they always did, knocking back huge quantities of spirits. Unknown to them, we too were drinking. The party was going smoothly until one of the Scottish girls, suddenly overwhelmed by the prospect of leaving her boyfriend of two weeks, became hysterical. People tried to calm her down, but her shrieks became increasingly loud until even the adults could no longer ignore them, and they came rushing down the stairs to see what was happening.

It was obvious that she had been drinking and they moved quickly into action to limit the damage. The party stopped at once and the girl, still clinging to her boyfriend, was driven off sobbing. While this was happening, two men were posted to stand on the lawn and wave reassuringly at any police patrol that might drive past. I was intrigued that the parents seemed as wary of the police as their children. I was used to policemen not noticing me unless I asked them for help.

When I said goodbye to the girl who had given me so much pleasure, there were tears in my eyes. She was politely sad, but I learned later that she went back to her boyfriend who worked at Friendlies Burger Bar. I had bought my own copy of *Wildflowers* which I played while writing airmail letters to her which I ended 'All my love'. Eventually there was nothing more to write and the correspondence dried up as I returned to life in a separate carriage.

The following year I had an opportunity for a further exchange, this time with a French family, the d'Hautefeuilles, who were in the champagne business. The connection was established by some friends, the Denholms, who ran a shipping business and lived not far from us in an Edwardian house with wooden panelled public rooms, large fireplaces and a sweeping drive at the front with a clay tennis court to the side. At the back of the house, a garden dropped steeply in curved tiers, falling away like an opera house viewed from the gods.

During the war Mr Denholm had for a time commanded the 603 Squadron of Spitfires known proudly as the City of Edinburgh Squadron. He never spoke of the war, but I knew from talk in the town that he had been involved with the capture of Rudolf Hess and had been shot down on several occasions during the Battle of Britain. On the sideboard in the dining room was a silver salver, inscribed 'Congratulations on the Hundredth Hun'. His first name was George and he had such an avuncular nature that Alasdair and I referred to him as 'Uncle George', though we never called him that to his face. It was only years later that I discovered from reading The Last Enemy by Richard Hilary that during the war, when he was in his early thirties, he had been given the same nickname.

The Denholms had had four successful exchanges with the d'Hautefeuilles but had then run out of children to swap, which is why they had suggested me. They often invited Alasdair and me to play tennis, after which we might stay on to have supper and play cards as a wood fire crackled in the hearth. I trusted their judgement. If they suggested an exchange, it would be a good one.

When Arnaud came to stay with us, we liked him immediately. He had a dignity that belied his age and an ability to accept any situation without being ruffled. When, on a trip back from the Trossachs, Alasdair drove into a sheep at fifty miles an hour and car slewed off the road into a hedge, he barely blinked before getting out of the car as one might leave a taxi at a station. Having taken stock of the situation, he lugged the sheep off the road and helped to push the car back onto the tarmac, before elegantly resuming his place in the front seat.

Sometimes his English could be startlingly advanced, as when we were driving through an anonymous town in the Lowland belt and he asked what the working population of the town might be. It was a curious question, but he was hoping to go to a Grande École in Paris where such esoteric knowledge is highly prized. After a quick discussion with

Alasdair, I told him it was about three thousand. Looking back on my answer now that I have a greater understanding of the Grande École system, I realise that in an entrance interview it would be deemed to be perfect, being based on nothing but confidence.

For the return match in France, I flew from Edinburgh to Le Touquet in a Caledonian Airways BAC 1-11, stepping onto the rain-soaked tarmac from the stairs that dropped from the back of the aircraft like a tail. Arnaud was waiting to meet me in a beige VW Beetle which had a removable magnetic 90 sign on the back wing, indicating that he was a newly qualified driver.

As we drove south-east across the flat land of Pas de Calais, he explained to me that we were going to their summer home that they only used in August. For the rest of the year it was shut up.

I had been expecting a country cottage, but as we passed a long high wall, he indicated that we had reached our destination. For a section of about fifty yards, the height of the wall dropped, allowing me to see the façade of a four-storey country house through railings. We continued until we reached the end of the wall where there was an entrance to a drive that looped back through a wood, emerging at the house.

Although I knew that the family business was making champagne, the reputation of their brand, Bollinger, meant nothing to me. On the first evening, in an attempt to make me welcome with easy conversation, they asked me to name as many champagne brands as I could. Thanks to the generosity of Pan-Am, I was able to answer Moët et

The d'Hautefeuille's summer house in Pas de Calais

Chandon, but then came to a halt. They found it hard to believe I had not heard of more and looked encouragingly at me as if they could will me to come up with answers. I was reduced to proffering sparkling wine brands that I had seen advertised in the *Sunday Times* colour supplement, though it was with the desperation of a fare dodger offering yesterday's ticket and they shook their heads sadly. At least I had the self-respect not to say Pomagne, a brand of premium cider dressed up like a sparkling wine, which we often drank on celebratory occasions at home.

The family dressed in the timeless style of France, with clothes of simple good quality, perfect fit and classic colours. Set against them, I was conspicuously out of place, with my long hair, clothes of poor cut in bright pastel colours and homemade jumpers. Fortunately, my prep school training allowed me to slip into their company without appearing gauche and however discordant they found my 1960s British clothing, they purred that I had style. My hair was another matter altogether and I was taken to a nearby town to have it cut.

Memory of the war was still raw. Monsieur d'Hautefeuille referred to the Germans as the Boche. The Boche had shot out the eyes of a woman in an oil painting on a panel above the fireplace in the salon. The Boche had parked their vehicles in the large walled garden. He showed me the imprint of a Boche boot in the concrete base of a military installation that had been turned into a tennis court. We went to the woods to see the V1 launch sites that the Boche had built. Germans were always Boche.

Not every mention of the Boche was bad. Thumping the VW Beetle with his fist on the roof to show its strength, he grudgingly admitted that the Boche made good cars. Much of his anti-Boche sentiment was to make a point about recent history for my benefit. Inside, I felt he had had enough of war.

Over the next four weeks I grew to admire the simplicity and formality of French family life. Meals were served at a large circular table, capable of seating twelve people with ease, with a lazy Susan in the centre. The formula was unchanging: crudités, salad, red meat or chicken or fish, Camembert – always Camembert – and fruit. With lunch and dinner there were baskets of sliced baguettes and supermarket red wine decanted from cartons into carafes and poured into tumblers. My happy notion that I would drink champagne with every meal proved wrong.

I noticed the physical contact that was part of their routine. Both on meeting at breakfast and on going to bed at night, the family members would kiss one another and shake hands with me. Compared with the carelessness of our offhand acknowledgements at home, the ritual of touch was a powerful reassurance that each gave to the other.

To my surprise, the children addressed their parents as 'vous', not just to be respectful but, as I later learned, because it was part of the stamp of the old establishment, as was their habit of referring to prices in old francs. Fortunately, they were forgiving of my universal use of the familiar 'tu' form, realising that in English, pronouns were not required to comment on degrees of reverence or friendship.

My lapses, although frequent, were not as bad as those of their New York distributor who used to call their aunt Lilli, 'old girl'. His impertinence was all the more amusing to them because in France she used to insist that her household staff speak to her in the third person – would Madame like?

Gestures were a sign of rank as much as language. When meeting older women, the boys took the woman's hand and raised to their lips. In the course of a practical lesson on the correct form of polite kissing, I announced to Madame d'Hautefeuille that I had just had sexual intercourse with her. Laughingly she exclaimed, 'Non, non! C'est une baise mais il faut dire embrasser!' I could tell by the embarrassed looks of everyone around me that I had said a powerfully bad thing. It was mystifying how a verb could take a respectable noun and turn it into a lout.

If generally the French were formally polite, they could also be surprisingly crude. At a show-jumping event at a nearby chateau, men would open their raincoats and urinate where they stood with as much lack of inhibition as the horses.

We saw a large number of chateaus because the d'Hautefeuilles's friends lived in them. Often, the houses were comfortably worn, with the formal areas closed off and the family living in a few rooms with rugs thrown over decaying upholstery and Bakelite valve wirelesses on sideboards. Grass was kept short not by mowers that left stripes, but by sheep that left droppings.

On three occasions I went with the family to soirées held in the grounds of nearby chateaus. The formula was always the same. A large tent was erected with a wooden floor for dancing. In the early evening, the guests would arrive in Citroen 2CVs, the car of choice, emerging with the panache of James Bond unzipping his wetsuit to reveal a dinner jacket.

Only two types of drink were served; whisky and champagne. After a dinner of exquisite finger food, the disco started, and the fabulous creatures set to in energetic rock and roll, throwing each other away, then pulling together and spinning round with a flair that made my unskilled shaking on the dancefloor seem lumpen.

All the hosts used the same party organiser, so every detail of the evening was the same, down the last record track and canapé. As the guest list never varied either, consisting as it did of a smart set who went to the Pas de Calais for the summer, the parties only differed in the chateau in whose grounds they were held.

I did not possess 'un smoking' but wore an ill-fitting dark blue suit from Burtons with an ordinary tie. My French, although of average standard for a British child after eight

A chateau belong to a friend of the d'Hautefeuille
family in Pas de Calais

years of study, was not fluent enough for me to hold even
a simple conversation. I used to stand by the side of the
tent trying to look engaged while drinking champagne,
intercepting whatever food came past and waiting for the
time to go home.

Being on my own and not speaking the language, I found
the days long, though they passed pleasantly. We played
carom billiards on a blue-felted table without pockets that
required every score to be a cannon. The table was covered
in fine dust from the woodworm that worked tirelessly to
eat the timbers in the ceiling beams. There was woodworm
everywhere. The creatures had much to eat because there
were bare wooden floors and wooden shutters. No one was
in the slightest concerned that, given time, they would eat

the house. At home, the discovery that a piece of furniture had woodworm led to it being burned within the hour.

The family were subtle in finding ways of diluting the heavy presence of an outside guest. I accompanied every trip to the supermarket which was half an hour away by car, and they encouraged me to go into the woods on my own to explore the V1 launch sites. When they learned that I could shoot, they lent me a 410 shotgun so that in the early evening I could take a pot at the rabbits in the garden. Whenever we drove past in the car, rabbits seemed so plentiful that they gave the illusion that the whole earth was a heaving mass of fur, but the moment I tried to kill them, they were nowhere to be seen. The gun had tiny cartridges the diameter of a disposable ballpoint pen and a short range, but despite that I always had hope that the next spin of the wheel would be a win. On the few occasions that I fired, the rabbits ran off unscathed, sometimes mockingly delaying their escape.

In the evenings after dinner we would retire to the drawing room and play bridge. Madame d'Hautefeuille always played, usually with two of the children and me. It was an ideal game, as we could all be part of a shared activity without my having to converse. Monsieur d'Hautefeuille would often be making phone calls in the background, a more alarming activity than it sounds because the French phone system at the time was notoriously unreliable and he would hurl the phone across the room in frustration. If my French had been up to the task, I might have suggested that had it been made by the Boche, the system would have worked.

The value of my French exchange was more successful culturally than it was linguistically because it gave me an understanding and love of France that has developed and endured.

The following Christmas, when I went on a school rugby trip to Narbonne in south-western France, I no longer felt a stranger when we arrived in Paris to change to the night train south. The Continent was in the grip of snow which was piled high in the streets as we emerged from the metro at Gare Austerlitz.

The teachers encouraged us to go off in small groups to find somewhere to eat. I went with three friends to a dark café I had found which was filled with national servicemen in uniform returning to base. The tables were laid with red gingham cloths on which were placed old wine bottles, cascading with wax that dripped down from the candles placed in their necks. Soon we were tucking into boeuf Bourguignonne, the plat du jour, served with a large carafe of red wine and baguette. I was pleased with myself for finding a place so obviously authentic. I was also pleased to be so comfortable in French surroundings that I felt I was welcoming my teammates as guests to my world.

In a more cautious age our teachers might have been worried that we could have got lost and missed the train or even that we would come to harm, but we were all old enough to drive cars and some of us were even old enough to fight for our country, so neither outcome was likely. The only real danger we had faced was that our appetite for independence might have been suppressed.

When we arrived in the south, we were surprised to learn that some of the pitches were covered in snow, though arrangements were quickly made to transfer those games to pitches that had been cleared.

A greater surprise was the strength of the teams we were playing. I had formed the idea that French boys would be rather small and smoke a great deal, a perception based on the profile of a French boy who had joined us for two years in the sixth form. I was soon disabused of this notion. The French rugby players were huge, and we lost every game we played.

The consolation for our losses was that we were royally entertained to an early supper after every game, often in large open spaces under the grandstands in the stadiums. There was always wine in quantity. After one match, our bus driver drank more than would have been wise had he been walking home. Fortunately, he was able to sit at the steering wheel which steadied him.

My final years at school were no more successful academically than the first. Though some teaching was excellent much of it was poor, with little emphasis being placed on thinking. Learning facts and being tested was how we approached most subjects.

Unsurprisingly, whenever presented with a question I always tried to remember what the answer ought to be instead of having the confidence to release the brake on my brain and let it work. The matter came to a head one weekend when Norman, in his attempt to help me with my History A level exam, asked me about Cromwell's foreign policy. I gave the usual halting reply of 'um' and 'er' until he interrupted me. What did a leader need for a foreign policy? An army and navy. What was the problem with any army or navy? Paying for it. How did you get the money to pay the soldiers? Taxation. Is taxation popular? No. There were many more questions but gradually, by getting me to think, Norman made me realise that I could structure an answer which would help tease out the facts. It was thanks to Norman that History was the only subject in which I achieved a respectable grade.

We were all required to join the Combined Cadet Force to get a taste of military discipline and give us a running start for a commission in the case of there being a call-up. The Naval Unit was popular with smokers because they could take the whaler out into the Forth away from prying eyes. The RAF section was thought to be a comfortable choice because nearly everything it did took place indoors. The army had the opposite reputation. Worse, people who had been on camp brought back stories of being awoken at first light by a sergeant major running his swagger stick along the corrugated iron wall of the Cultybraggan Nissen huts.

I joined the RAF section and every Monday morning in term time caught the bus, proudly wearing my uniform of scratchy blue wool and a shirt with a detachable starched collar. My pride was real. Memory of the war was still recent, though distant enough for time to have chipped away the terror of aerial combat and bombing missions. What was left, at least for non-participants, was a gleaming casting of bravery and success. Films *like Reach for the Sky, The Dambusters, 633 Squadron* and *The Battle of Britain* were filled with a glamour that I felt shone on me when I put on an RAF uniform, even that of a schoolboy cadet.

Our prized possession was a glider, not unlike the Colditz glider in sophistication, and kept with similar secrecy in a hut on our playing fields. From time to time it would be brought out and dragged downwind, where its tail would be attached by a release mechanism to a stake driven into the ground and a long V-shaped bungee attached to a hook under its nose. A small cadet would be appointed to be the pilot and take his seat in the exposed cockpit, holding the control column in his hand and putting his feet on the rudder pedals. The remaining cadets would pull both ends of the bungee until their heels began to slip on the grass and they could pull no more, at which point the pilot would release the glider from the stake and it would lumber forward.

Whenever I pulled on the bungee, I was motivated by the hope that we might be able to impale the glider and its smug little pilot on the pointed railings that surrounded the field, but for a flight of that length the glider needed more power than the bungee could provide and only ever took to the air for a few yards before landing on its skid.

At Easter 1969 we went to RAF Leuchars, which had a squadron of English Electric Lightnings, one of the best interceptors ever built because of its extraordinary ability to go into a vertical climb like a rocket. For some reason, *The Scotsman* thought our visit was worth a photograph on the front page, possibly because the date was 1 April. I was lucky enough to watch a display arranged for some very senior officers. While spectacular, it lasted only a short time because that was how long the fuel lasted. If a Lightning were ever intercepting a Russian bomber, the attack would have to be executed more like a clay pigeon shoot than a ride to hounds.

The Lightning flight simulator on which pilots were trained had at its heart a huge version of a classroom roller blackboard on which had been built a model of the countryside and airfield. As the countryside spun on the belt, a television camera filmed it, the angles, heights and speeds being linked to inputs from the controls in the simulator cockpit. The film was then projected in front of the pilot. Although the simulator was highly sophisticated, it was still crude enough to require a dual version of the aircraft to be built for training purposes.

At that time all RAF pilots were men. Women might be air traffic controllers, but beyond that they weren't allowed to play with the toys. As a 'Look at Life' film of the period crowed proudly, 'In today's modern RAF, a girl can do any job a man can do, that is except navigate or fly an aircraft.'

There was a naïvety to the safety posters in the hangars, which assumed that men would only pay attention to messages communicated in sexual terms. A typical one warned of the danger of walking into propellers by telling men to remember that 'Props are like birds. They're here to stay but don't lose your head!'

It never struck me as strange that no women flew, it being an immutable law of nature that flying was for chaps. Girls were there to support.

As I approached my final year, I had to make a decision about where to go to university. Alasdair had followed Norman to Cambridge and my parents felt I had the ability to go too. They paid for me to take the sleeper to London and spend a weekend with him in the hope that being in Cambridge might ignite my interest and give me the incentive to win a place at the university.

I wandered Cambridge in the grey half-light of a winter day, absorbing the beauty of a city where every generation had had an opportunity to dig deep into its pockets and show the best it could build. In between the colleges, the streets snaked like grouting, lined with buildings which displayed their style, not with the dinner-jacketed uniformity of Edinburgh, but with the individuality of women in evening dress, each oblivious to the taste of its neighbour and together providing variety and colour. From the central hub, lines of simple terraced houses grew like crystals in random formations, their streets punctuated with the shops and pubs that beat with the pulse of the community. If there was a place I could love as much as Winchester, this was it.

In the afternoon, Alasdair took me to have sherry with his tutor in his rooms at Pembroke, where a gas fire hissed. His tutor must have drunk a few sherries before we arrived, or downed a pint or two of lunchtime claret, or even done both, because he lolled back in his wing chair, his head rolling from side to side as if trying to find a comfortable position for sleep.

The trip succeeded beyond my parents' wishes. I could see myself as an undergraduate with my head buried in books, showing an enthusiasm for learning that I had yet to reveal. Sadly, it was a love filled with the same hopelessness I had felt on seeing the girl on the bus to school.

Back home, I would go to my room with the intent of working but would give up in frustration because I had no idea how to go about it. I still regarded academic work as if it was like digging a potato bed rather than setting off on an exploration. Apart from in History, my results in class never improved. Meanwhile the school had decided that I was not particularly bright but worked hard, so it was unwilling to support me in applying for Cambridge. Instead I applied to Bristol University to read law and was given a conditional offer.

In my last year I had been elected secretary of the debating society, which introduced me to the joy of being able to write comic caricatures of people's contributions. I discovered as I read the minutes out every week that I could use words to make people laugh, something that gave me more satisfaction than anything else.

When my A level results came through, my results were so poor that all thought of returning to England was lost. I cannot put all the blame on my teachers. I did not apply myself. I bought summaries of my English texts instead of reading them. Some of my History books were virginal when I came to sell them second hand. I read my French texts in English translation. I was not an industrious pupil.

Was I idle because I was disengaged or was I disengaged because I was idle? Would it have made a difference if my birthday had been a few days later, so that I would have benefited from being the oldest person in the year group and not the youngest? The answers are irrelevant. Life cannot be re-run so there is no lesson to be learned. There is only one person who is responsible for what we do in our lives and we all start with a mixture of good cards and bad. Mine had been mostly good.

I left the school without sadness. I had made good friends and been happy, but I had never formed an attachment with it, nor it with me, because we were both seeking things that the other did not offer. When I look back on my school reports, those of my prep school were full of promise and expectation of high achievement, while those of my day school sighed with despair at my lack of ability and progress. My choice of school had not been a good fit.

Had it been a marriage, we should have needed counselling or even divorced.

Over thirty years later, I was invited to a dinner of old boys in the Caledonian Club in London, otherwise known as the Scottish Embassy. It was the only event of its kind I have ever attended and will be the last, as I found it hard to relate to the old men who were in tears as they recalled what the school had meant to them.

CHAPTER 7

University

There were about a hundred of us, sitting in rows on what looked like church pews with flat surfaces to write on, large enough to take a writing pad. A man came into the room and without introduction started to speak about Marcus taking Aurelius's wine and mixing it with his own honey to make mead.

To begin with I thought the lecturer's extraordinarily slow speech resulted from him taking an exaggerated view of the pauses needed in a public delivery, but then to my horror I saw my fellow students writing down in longhand every word he was saying. I was back in my first form at prep school, taking dictation from the teacher.

It was my first law lecture at Aberdeen University and was on the subject of Roman law. It might have been helpful had the lecturer explained why Roman law might be relevant to a Scottish lawyer, but we were not to be let in on that secret. Instead we had landed on the Normandy beaches with no understanding of why we were there.

It seemed beyond comprehension that we were not given mimeographed copies of the notes, allowing the lecturers to talk round their subjects and bring them alive. A time and motion study expert would have declared the lectures a redundant process, but such logic did not prevail. We made our protest, which was ignored; as we later learned protests were made and ignored every year.

The logical way of countering the law faculty's intransigence would have been to send a single student with good handwriting to the lectures and then distribute copies of his or her notes, but the faculty was wise to this. An attendance list was passed round and anyone who did not attend the lectures was not allowed to sit the exams.

To make matters worse, we were expected to read any case that was referenced in the lecture, yet there were only three copies of the cases and over a hundred of us.

There were no regular tutorials to spur us to action, although once or twice a year one would be arranged at which the participants, unused to giving an opinion, stared at the floor while the lecturer tried to stimulate interest. Essays too were rarely requested; marking that number of scripts would have been an imposition on people more interested in academic research. The stark reality was that the way to pass the course was to take the dictation, read the rubric summaries of the cases (if even that were possible) and then regurgitate what we had half-remembered at the year-end exams.

By the end of the first week, I realised that university was not going to stir my interest, far less ignite it. My blood boiled with frustration and being only just eighteen, I lacked the maturity to deal with it.

I had decided to go to Aberdeen University with all the enthusiasm of someone offering to dance with the last person without a partner. Going there felt like the price of failure. My A levels had failed to meet an offer I had from Bristol by one grade and because my highest grade was only a B, Cambridge was out of the question. Fortunately, I had achieved A grades in my Scottish Higher exams which were of a less demanding standard, so Aberdeen accepted me.

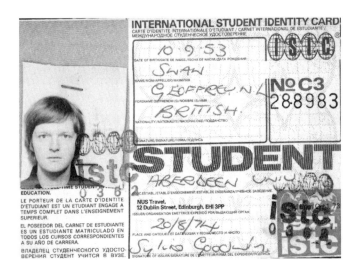

I lived in a hall of residence in Old Aberdeen, just off a cobbled street lined with terraced Georgian houses that must have been noted in the little black book of any film location company. The hall of residence was a 1960s design of little box rooms in an accommodation block with a round central core containing all the public rooms. The residential block had two wings – one for men and the other for women – linked by covered walkways to the central complex. The sexes were allowed free movement between the two wings until 10pm when they had to retire to their own quarters like school rugby players at half time.

For the first time in my life since the age of seven, I lived with girls. After two fallow years since Massachusetts, I should have thrown myself into an orgy of sexual discovery, but I held back, placing girls on a pedestal and imagining every contact was a prelude to marriage. I should have remembered from my experience on the bus from New York that sometimes girls didn't even want conversation.

I did have partial success, invariably at parties in the hall of residence when I had more luck than I deserved. After drinking too much and dancing too closely, I would go back to a girl's room for what is often described with excruciating coyness as heavy petting, usually a clumsy affair as I was unfamiliar with female anatomy. I also underestimated the importance of winning the mind, assuming that women responded to crude stimulation as easily as men.

While my performance as an apprentice lover was shambolic, a far greater failing was not to have developed affairs that lasted for weeks rather than hours, but I never understood that each ephemeral relationship was another apprentice's pot, thrown to be broken.

The social segregation I had grown up with was a further inhibition, as I had a strong desire to stay within my group which I defined at a higher level than an outsider might have done, largely because it was set in my mind at an early age. If asked to specify my ideal girlfriend, she would have been one of John William Waterhouse's water nymphs from a good family in the Home Counties with a received pronunciation accent and a sharp wit. Unsurprisingly, they were few and far between and I could find none in Aberdeen.

My confused view of my social position might explain why, on arrival in Aberdeen, I had been so affected by Joseph Losey's film of *The Go-Between* which filled me with an overpowering wistfulness. I wanted to return to the cinema to watch it repeatedly, as an escape from reality. I even bought the book and read it in a day, an untold feat for one who normally read slowly, often leaving books unfinished. Aside from the clandestine relationship and the magic, I felt I had much in common with Leo Colston. I too had been brought up in a modest middle-class family but had been able to blend in with a grander family for a summer and, like him, I had unwittingly tripped over minor shibboleths. But the greatest similarity was that I was haunted by a reproach from a younger self that I had squandered a good start. In my case it had been by a succession of failures which resulted in my being expelled from an England I loved and ended up with my living in a small characterless room, leaving every morning to take dictation at an institution I did not value.

If I found the law course less than exciting, it had the benefit that lectures were only held in the morning four days a week, Fridays being free, so I had a great deal of free time. In order to occupy myself, I joined the University Air Squadron so that I could learn to fly.

The application process was straightforward. I sent off a form and shortly afterwards received a letter inviting me to go for interview, typed in the unmistakeable government font on a small piece of paper so old and yellowed it must have come from stock ordered well before the Munich crisis.

My hair was long, which was not unusual. Most boys at university grew hair to their shoulders and those who did not were either thought to be slightly odd or be in the military. I decided to get mine cut. While that decision was sensible, sending away for a razor comb that I had seen advertised in the small ads of *Private Eye* was not. The benefits of the device, much heralded in the copy, was that I would never have to pay to get my hair cut again and could thin it as naturally as combing it. It was an investment with an immediate payback.

When it arrived, I unpacked it excitedly and drew it, not through the back of my hair as a discreet test, but through my forelock, which it removed in a single chunk. There was no question of it thinning anything. The hair at the front of my head was cut to a stump the width of the device, which was considerable. I stared at it in horror, hardly daring to leave my room and let others see me. The only thing to be done was to go to the barber and pay for him to do his best to remedy the damage. It was a comparatively painless introduction to the wisdom that a financial proposition sounding too good to be true should be left to others to profit from.

I arrived at the interview with hair shorter than it needed to have been. In the conversation with the squadron leader who commanded the unit, I managed to get across my fascination with flight, my experience with the CCF and the leadership positions I had had at school. It must have been as convincing a plea as any other because they accepted me, subject to being fit for service.

The medical was a few days later at the squadron headquarters. An orderly went through a health form with me, carefully keeping control of the pen in case I should write anything I might regret. We were making good progress when he asked if I suffered from hay fever. Hay fever sounded innocuous, so I answered truthfully that I did. He asked if it was mild. I could remember it being so severe that on my exchange in France I had difficulty breathing in the night. I told him it was quite mild. He seemed relieved and said that he would put down that I didn't suffer from it, otherwise I would fail.

Next, I went down into the basement for a more thorough examination by an RAF doctor who measured my limbs and tested my hearing using a crude system of whispering words ever more quietly as he wandered round the room. To begin with he used numbers, but then he said 'sister'. I assumed he was saying 'sixteen' so repeated this back to him. We had this exchange three times until in desperation I said it sounded much more like sister than sixteen, at which point he appeared relieved.

I was nervous about the final part of the medical, because existing squadron members had told me about it. It was an experience requiring me first to lie on an examination table, naked but for my underpants, while every reflex was tormented. Then the pants were pulled down and the indignity of the other checks completed.

Over the winter holiday I learned the phonetic alphabet and in early January went up to Aberdeen in the week before the start of term for my first flight instruction in a de Havilland Chipmunk, by then nearing the end of its life as a basic trainer. It was a pretty aircraft with a fixed undercarriage and a tail wheel. Though it looked delicate, it was tough enough to survive the shocks that students inflicted on it. The dictum was that it was an easy aircraft to fly but a hard aircraft to fly well. Before I flew, I had a briefing from my instructor in the squadron hut and put on my Mae West life jacket before slipping into my parachute harness. The parachute itself hung like a rabbit's tail and became the padded cushion I sat on in the metal bucket seat of the cockpit. The helmet came in two parts. The soft inner lining with a headset and a rubber mouthpiece with a microphone was of the type worn by crews in films of the Second World War. The 'bone dome' or hard outer shell with a green-tinted visor was a post-war development to protect pilots' heads from a variety of different assaults.

After we waddled out to the aircraft my instructor showed me the external pre-flight checks and then slid back the canopy. I climbed up the wing root into the front seat and my instructor got in the back while the ground crew helped me to strap in.

I had been on air experience flights in a Chipmunk in the CCF, so was not unfamiliar with it, though there was a big difference between being a passenger and being instructed.

After an exchange with air traffic control which to me was unintelligible, we were off. Being unable to see directly ahead of us because the engine cowling blocked our view, we snaked our way along the taxiway using the rudder bar to apply the brakes first on one wheel and then on another.

The lessons all now blur into one, but we started with upper air work, first learning the effects of control and how to make balanced turns, then slowing the aircraft to recognise the wallowing and floppiness of the controls that warn of a stall that could kill at low altitude. So deeply was the fear of the stall instilled that I still become alert on a commercial jet if it wallows on final approach and I can't help wanting to put my hand on the thrust levers, ready to apply power. After stalling we did spins where we spiralled towards the ground like a sycamore leaf with one wing stalled and the other not. As a break between exercises on the effects of control, my instructor performed barrel rolls, loops and stall turns.

One of his favourite manoeuvres at the end of a flight was to ask permission for the control tower to do a run and break. We would fly fast at low level above the runway in the opposite direction to the one in which we were intending to land. When we reached the far end, he would lift the nose to gain height and lose speed, turn tightly, apply full flap and do a gentle three-point landing.

He was fond of dogfights and, if we came across another instructor – though not the chief flying instructor who would be obliged to take a dim view of a combat manoeuvre in non-combat aircraft – they would try to out-turn each other, an exercise which gave me a feeling of what fighting must have been like in the war. I could understand only too easily why pilots became fatally attracted to the aircraft they were trying to shoot down.

With each trip that we did, I followed through on the take-offs and landings, listening to my instructor as he hummed to himself to keep me calm. Taking off was the highlight of each trip and nothing equalled the excitement of turning onto the runway and lining up with the dotted white centre line that cut through the pool of black scrub marks at the touchdown point. As I opened the throttle wide, the perfection of symmetry, coordination and power was thrilling.

Landing had its challenges. As you crossed the threshold of the runway, you had to close the throttle and pull back on the control column just as the wheels were about to touch the tarmac in the start of what was known as the flare. As the speed dropped off, you gradually pulled the nose higher and higher as you pretended you were going to be able to fly to the end of the runway. Eventually the airspeed would be so low that the aircraft could no longer sustain flight and it would settle on its three wheels from a height of a few inches, the much wished for 'three-point landing'.

There were many ways of getting a landing wrong. The most common was to start the flare too late so that the mainwheels bounced hard, sending you back up in the air again. Another was to lift the nose too high after closing the throttle while you still had enough speed to gain altitude. You then had to decide if the ballooning was sufficiently mild for you to hold the stick back and wait for the aircraft to slam down hard on the runway, sometimes landing on the tailwheel first, or whether you were so high that you had to apply power and abandon that approach.

Shortly after Easter at Aberdeen Dyce Airport on a still, grey day with high cloud, I flew my first solo. I had been practising circuits when my instructor got out and gave me my own call sign, Kilo Golf Sierra Six Zero, the military using personal rather than aircraft call signs for identification.

It was liberating not having someone breathing down my neck, so much so that I began drifting above circuit height on the downwind leg and it took a moment or two for me to concentrate and bring myself back down to 1,000 feet. The landing was unusually smooth, though on two wheels, not three. When the man in the control tower said, 'Very nice Kilo Six Zero. Welcome to the club,' I felt terrific.

This Is To Certify that

CDT. PLT. SWAN

a member of
Aberdeen University Air Squadron
has today successfully completed his

FIRST SOLO FLIGHT

in a Chipmunk J Mk. 10 Aircraft
at Aberdeen - Dyce Airport

19 MAY 72
date

Officer Commanding
Aberdeen University Air Squadron

By custom, I was supposed to celebrate my first solo by drinking a 'Night Fighter' in a single go. It was a vile drink consisting of a measure of port for the port light, crème de menthe for the starboard light, vodka for the strobe and gin for the landing light, all topped up with Guinness for the bat black night. I had seen many people sick after drinking it, so I didn't ask for one and no one bought me one. Receiving my blue and yellow squadron scarf which I was now entitled to wear at the neck of my flying suit meant much more than a poisoning.

In the summer holiday the squadron aircraft were flown by the more experienced members down to RAF Bicester where we had concentrated flying for two weeks. I had bought a copy of *Bomber* by Len Deighton and tried to imagine what it would feel like if we had all been born thirty years earlier. The idea of flying at night across Europe, even without people trying to kill me, was far beyond anything I thought I would be capable of doing. How could they sleep with their heads filled with images of the way they could die, and their bodies primed with adrenaline? How could they cycle through the English countryside knowing what they would face in the night? And yet for all the shared danger, Deighton wrote of the niggles and bullying that were part of life: the placing of an axe with a new crew to suggest they were for the chop; or the refusal by the more experienced members to recognise them until they had proved themselves. I was beginning to have a slight insight as to how that could happen. Our training, simple and safe though it was, was still demanding. For the bomber crews, the task of preparing themselves for the night's raid will have been so demanding that their tolerance for others will have been low.

One thing we had in common with wartime squadrons was a taste for rowdy parties. Anyone who didn't drink or went to bed too soon received a dressing down from the boss. Heavy drinking was an important part of squadron morale.

Early on in the camp we organised a dance and invited some nurses from Arthur Sanctuary in Oxford. One of them, who was similar in enthusiasm to the girl I had met on my American exchange, attached herself to me in a tight embrace which we maintained all night. The squadron decided the party had been so good that we would have another one the following night, so the girl and I arranged to meet again. Sadly, I was delayed and by the time I arrived, she was closely clinched with someone else. Yet again, I had been presented with evidence that teenage girls are not seeking marriage and yet again I failed to notice.

If I was still floundering around with girls, my relationships with my own sex were much more assured. In an early letter written to my parents shortly after I arrived at university, I had written, 'A boy I have met from Glenalmond [school] and I are thinking of playing rugger for one of the teams.' The boy, Mike Risk, and I were to have a lifelong friendship until his sudden, natural death twenty years later.

We were both reading law and lived in the same student hall of residence. He had been working as a busboy in the restaurant of Jasper Park Lodge in Alberta, living with a girl he had met there and to whom he wrote long airmail letters every week. He had an excitement for life which was contagious and a personality that attracted people and opened doors. He amplified my virtues, teased me for my deficiencies and had social connections that spread throughout Scotland.

It was the last strong relationship with my own sex, made more intense on my part by an ember still smouldering under the ash of childhood. But it was not an ember I wanted to breathe to flame. I was content to feel its heat and let it die.

Mike was an example of someone who had not been emotionally handicapped by being at a single-sex boarding school, partly because he had only started to board aged thirteen and partly because he had a web of female cousins and friends he had grown up with. He adored girls as they adored him. For me, he was the guide I needed as I blundered my way from adolescence into adulthood.

At the end of the first year, he went back to Jasper where he worked all summer. The following year, his girlfriend flew over from Canada but before she arrived, he and I went on an InterRail trip to the Continent. With our ex-army backpacks, sleeping bags and a flysheet for cover, we set off to Paris and then south to Provence before heading into Spain to see the running of the bulls in Pamplona. We then retraced our steps, continuing to northern Italy, thence through Switzerland to northern France and home.

The route made little logistical sense, and was the product of choices made hastily, often with a desire to temper adventure with the familiar, as in my case the decision to go to Avignon and in Mike's the desire to return to Sanary, where he had had family holidays. Sometimes, as when we ended up in Barcelona instead of Pamplona, our destination was decided for us as a result of our getting into the wrong section of a train.

In Spain, Franco was still head of state and there was a feeling that people were careful. Neither of us spoke Spanish nor did we know a great deal of the culture beyond what I had absorbed from Miss Brewis's magic lantern shows. Yet when we got out of the train in Hendaye, having crossed the border back into France, it was as if we had been let out of school for the holidays. Unaware that we had been oppressed, we suddenly felt free.

In Venice we slept outside the station, believing that we were doing something daringly original. When I awoke briefly at midnight, I found we were surrounded by hundreds of other backpackers. A few hours later, we were woken by the police and moved on, wandering the streets at first light as we waited for the shops to open, the time passing with agonising slowness. My spirits were lowered by the discovery that a Fuji camera that had belonged to Norman had been stolen from under my head when I slept.

In Florence we were advised by the tourist office to catch a bus to a campsite in Fiesole where we met two English girls, Jackie and Caroline, who had driven to Italy in their Mini. Their laconic and frank conversation was the badge of girls of smart pedigree who had never bent to the will of authority or the rules of gentility. It would not have surprised me if at some stage in their school careers their parents had been summoned to see the headmistress.

As the Mini shuffled its way into Florence in heavy evening traffic, one or other of the girls would slide open a window and shout at a startled young Italian man that he should stop playing with himself.

If their behaviour was belligerent, it was as nothing compared with the aggressive attention that they received as blonde women. As we walked through the city, they invited us to drop back twenty paces and witness what it was like to be the bait. Wherever they went, men detached themselves and, muttering 'Bella! Bella!', slipped into their wake to join all the others who were also following, waiting for the moment to move in with a proposition. Later, in a carpark high above the city, the girls arranged for Mike and me to stand in the shadows while they returned to the car. Men were holding onto the door handles as they drove off, accelerating hard before screeching to a halt where we were standing, allowing us to pile in.

The girls had few illusions about the morals of Italian men. Whenever the Mini was parked, they removed the windscreen wiper blades and hid them inside the car. Nothing was left in view. I wished I had met them before I lost my camera.

We left the girls reluctantly before heading up to Switzerland where we joined a Swiss girl, Barbara Maier, who was at university us, staying both at her parents' home in Schaffhausen and at her grandmother's house by a lake that formed the border with Germany. I did not realise she was waving at me from the other railway carriage.

The first Christmas I went back home, I drove the Renault 12 that my parents had just bought on my recommendation, their first foreign car after a succession of Cortinas and a Vauxhall 2000. I had taken to buying Car magazine instead of the more traditional Motor and Autocar. It took an iconoclastic approach to motor journalism, forgoing advertising revenue in order to give unbiased views of the cars they were given to test and challenging our assumptions that British was best, often with damning reviews.

The Renault might have looked unorthodox with its concave rear window, but it was superior to the previous cars in every respect. Neither my parents nor I ever bought a British car again.

I stayed in the Air Squadron until my second year, when I resigned to stand for the position of president of the Debating Society, running against Alistair Darling, the future chancellor of the exchequer. I had realised that I was not going to join the RAF as a career, nor was I going to be able to obtain a licence, given that the military required more hours than I would be able to put in. Even if I could obtain one, I would not be able to afford to maintain it. By flying solo, I felt I had achieved a simple ambition of taking a heavier than air machine up into the sky by myself and, more importantly, bringing it down to land in one piece.

Fortunately for me, Alistair Darling's candidature was tainted by his association with the Socialist Society which put off voters who feared quite needlessly, though at my encouragement, that he would turn the debates into hectoring political rants. I was elected president, which entitled me to a large room in the universities administrative block, adorned with fading posters and newspaper cuttings, mostly connected with marches against injustices of different sorts.

I had a budget that I had to spend every term on pain of having it reduced, a basic concept that I found hard to understand because it discouraged thrift. Its main purpose was to pay the expenses of visiting speakers, allowing me to entertain them to dinner before the debate.

There was one debate a month. After deciding the question, we had to invite speakers and then advertise the event by designing posters and flyposting them in the dark, occasionally coming to the attention of the police.

Twice we decided to organise a great event in the main hall that accommodated hundreds of people and invite a panel of people to discuss a significant issue of the day. One of these was on the impact of North Sea oil that was just beginning to come on stream.

The pre-publicity was effective beyond anyone's expectations and rivers of people flowed in. I was chairman of the discussion and was both nervous and slightly drunk from the pre-meeting dinner. I had not been curious to find out what the role of a chairman might be and thought I fired a starting gun to set the speakers off to let them argue amongst themselves. As a result, I never challenged, or brought points together, or invited people to contribute. My performance was disastrous, and I crawled back to my room afterwards, hoping no one would have noticed. Some weeks later, I was talking with someone from the faculty who, not realising my role, said he had heard the meeting had been very badly chaired.

In my last Easter holiday, Mike and I were invited by my Swiss friend, Barbara, to go skiing in Pontresina, near St Moritz. We caught an overnight train from Glasgow to London, sleeping on the bench seats of an old corridor carriage.

The journey was not without incident. There was a gale blowing in the English Channel and throughout the crossing we could see only sky out of the windows on the starboard side and breaking waves and foam out of the windows on the port side. People around us were being sick.

As the night train to Basel was pulling out of Brussels station, a man who was running to climb into our carriage fell under the wheels. Although we could not see him, we could hear the shrieks of onlookers and see them covering their eyes and ears and turning away. The train carried on to a suburban station where it was stopped while the police came to look at the carriage, before letting us continue on our way.

That night our compartment filled with an Italian family who enjoyed a lavish picnic, the father being fed by his wife as if he were a baby, a sight I found revolting. Mike could sleep anywhere, snoring contentedly. I sat up all night feeling resentful.

We changed onto a narrow-gauge track for the last part of the journey to Samedan station. It was my first experience of a winter holiday abroad and I was struck by the brightness of the light as the sun reflected on the snow which lay deeply all around. Barbara met us in her car and drove us to her parents' chalet where the three of us were staying on our own.

Mike and Barbara were both good skiers and had their own equipment. I was a novice and had hired equipment from the university. On the first day we all went up to a gentle slope just above St Moritz where they hoped I might learn a snowplough. Somewhat to their consternation, they discovered that however steep the slope, my skis would not slide. In desperation, they took an arm each and pulled, setting me off with a trail of rust streaks in the snow behind me.

It was an unsatisfactory day, made more unsatisfactory when I discovered that the Ambre Solaire oil I had saved from my InterRail trip the previous year was a wholly inadequate barrier to sun reflected off snow at high altitude. By evening my face had swollen and my eyes were closed. That night, Barbara made a cut-out mask from a handkerchief which she stitched into my balaclava, creating a complete barrier from the sun.

For the first week, I skied in ski school as the masked man. For the second week I skied with the other two, holding them back as I stopped nervously at the top of every slope.

I still remained unaware until towards the end of the fourteen days we spent together that Barbara was trying to wave at me from the railway carriage. Had I met her when I had the maturity to appreciate what an exceptional person she was, I would have realised how fortunate I was that she liked me, but I was an immature boy, still dreaming of water nymphs. We kissed one evening while Mike slept in a chair in the corner of the room but the following day I behaved as if nothing had happened and the mood chilled.

We paid for the ski lifts by buying cards with numbers round the edges that were clipped by a man as we passed the entrance. For a long lift they would clip four or five numbers, but for a short button lift, only one. On the last day, we had done our last descent when I noticed that I still had enough points for us all to do another run. It seemed a pity to waste them.

Not long afterwards, I lay strapped in the rescue sledge being taken fast down the fall line of the slope, with the bones in my broken leg grating painfully at every movement. I had fallen in a fast schuss, a tip of one ski had dug in and the binding of my university ski club skis had not released. The rust streaks on the first day should have warned me of the quality of skis that I had hired.

I was taken to hospital in the back of a taxi with two doors. It was late on a Friday afternoon and there was a discussion about whether or not I should have to wait until the Monday for an operation on my leg, but Barbara's parents had some influence and the surgeon kindly agreed to operate. That night he fixed the bone with a plate and sixteen screws.

I woke up after the operation to find myself in an open ward with six others. At dawn a nurse came in, as she was to do every day, and said sweetly, 'Guten Tag! Bon jour! Buongiorno! Good morning!' as she made her way across the ward to the bed diagonally opposite me to tickle Bonetti, an Italian who had broken most of the bones in his body by falling into a river while repairing a bridge. He must have been recovering well because his multi-coloured bed socks would start to kick from under his bedclothes as he giggled.

In the bed immediately opposite me was a one-legged alcoholic in his mid-sixties called Herr Douch who was often sick from drinking too much red wine. Our Tibetan orderly removed the wine bottle whenever he saw it but Herr Douch always found more. In desperation, the orderly first confiscated Herr Douch's wooden leg and then put up sides to his bed like a baby's cot, but still Herr Douch remained happily intoxicated for most of the day.

The answer to the mystery was that Bonetti, who by this time could spin around in a wheelchair, used to find it for him, though how he did it, I never discovered. My world ended at the door to the ward.

In the bed next to me was a restaurant waiter who had injured his leg skiing, though he maintained that he had fallen down the stairs at work. No one believed him but everyone colluded. There was nothing to be gained by throwing sand in the cogs of an insurance claim.

I had no external splint on my leg, which meant I was spared itching that I could not scratch and could have a bath as soon as the skin had healed. The leg was comfortable for as long as I lay in bed but was agonising when I swung it into the vertical, as I was encouraged to do. It took over a week until I was able to achieve every patient's ambition of going to a flushing toilet. Until then I had to use a bedpan, an indignity made worse by the lack of curtains between the beds. Forced into action by a purgative, and mortally embarrassed, I adopted an ostrich's approach and held up the Times like a barricade at those moments.

Barbara and her parents were kind to me to a degree that went beyond anything I deserved, bringing me books and newspapers and making travel arrangements. In due course

I travelled by train First Class to Zurich and then by a BEA flight to Edinburgh and home. Although I had insurance, I never saw a single bill for anything.

Whenever I think of Barbara, I realise how badly I had behaved, but my excuse was that I still had a great deal to learn. To make matters worse, when I received a wedding invitation from her some years later, I wasn't sure what to do and, in my hesitation, did the one thing that no one should ever do and failed to reply. At that point I had smashed the vase beyond repair.

I still had the year-end exams to sit in May and followed my normal pattern of desperately trying to cram a year's work into a single day and then not sleeping as my mind raced in panic through the night. Fortunately, I passed.

At our year group farewell party, one of the lecturers in a moment of candour remarked on my ability to answer exam questions with just enough information to justify a pass mark of 50% but not enough to merit any more. When I tried to apologise for this lean performance, he congratulated me on my economy of effort.

The one subject in which I excelled and was interviewed for a distinction for was forensic medicine. It was undertaken by an elderly pathologist at the Royal Infirmary whose lectures were memorably illustrated with horrifying slides and brought alive by his graphic turn of phrase. He could easily have killed the subject by dictating his notes to us but fortunately for us, he did his job.

With my law degree in my pocket as evidence that I was a fit and proper person to be a solicitor, I left Aberdeen ready to take up my apprenticeship in Edinburgh. The position had not been easy to obtain, as every application I had made had been turned down. Luckily for me – or so I thought at the time – the father of an old school friend, hearing of my plight, invited me to become an apprentice at his firm.

It was a kindly act of nepotism but like a government grant to a company in a failing industry, it only postponed the inevitable. I had no formal training during my apprenticeship, so I was unable to build on the shallow foundations of knowledge I had acquired at university. For over eight years I struggled but with no solid grasp of the law, my reputation steadily declined. I found it hard to cope with failing because I did not see myself as a failure. I knew I had to rescue the situation.

My father had been right when he told me after the diving competition at my prep school that I should always remember that I was capable of more than I thought I was. It was a sound lesson to learn, though a more practical one might have been that however deeply I plunged, I always came up again. Shortly before my twenty-ninth birthday, I decided to take my career by the scruff of its neck. For the first time in my adult life, I stopped going down and saw the light above me. I kicked hard and shot towards the surface.